ANGELS IN MOURNING

ANGELS IN MOURNING

Sublime Madness, Ennui and Melancholy
in Modern Thought

Roger Bartra

REAKTION BOOKS

Published by
Reaktion Books Ltd
Unit 32, Waterside
44–48 Wharf Road
London N1 7UX, UK
www.reaktionbooks.co.uk

First published by Reaktion Books in 2018

English translation by Nick Caistor
Translation © Reaktion Books 2018

El duelo de los ángeles © 2004 by Roger Bartra
First published in Spain by Pre-Textos (Valencia) and in Mexico
by Fondo de Cultura Económica (Mexico City)

Printed and bound in Great Britain
by TJ International, Padstow, Cornwall

A catalogue record for this book is available from the British Library

ISBN 978 1 78023 972 9

Contents

PROLOGUE

In this book I have sought to explain how three lucid European thinkers peered into the abyss of chaos and irrationality. By looking at Immanuel Kant, Max Weber and Walter Benjamin I wanted to conduct a kind of anthropological experiment: to draw attention to some apparently marginal aspects of their thought in order to illuminate the way in which they gazed into darkness. This darkness is symbolized by the idea of melancholy, an ancient notion that is a keystone of modern Western culture. It is not easy to understand how melancholy, that symbol of imbalance and death, found a space in modern society. Why does this threatening expression of irrationality and mental disorder succeed in gaining a foothold at the very heart of a European culture guided by rationalism? It is possible that part of the explanation may lie in the blossoming of Romanticism, that deep-seated protest against both the Enlightenment and the capitalist order. But it was not only in the Romantic tradition that melancholy occupied a privileged position; it also took root in other cultural movements before and after it. In order to examine this question I have preferred to situate it outside the context of anti-modern Romanticism, and to study the way in which Enlightenment thought, modern social science and critical thinking have reacted to the feeling and idea of melancholy and its lengthy tail of ennui: apathy, madness, *spleen*, boredom, depression, mourning, disgust, chaos, sublime horror, existential nausea . . .

It is undeniable that the currents in which Kant, Weber and Benjamin were immersed were reluctant to openly regard those dark areas in which a radical melancholy otherness was concealed. Modern enlightened thought seldom considers darkness, and often denies it. Kant, Weber and Benjamin were not Romantic visionaries capable of finding their way among the shady regions of irrationality. And yet their blindness, their procedures and their stumbles help us illuminate – or at least delimit – those obscure areas that were invisible to them. My experiment consists in using as guide dogs three blind thinkers unable to see the dark face of the angel of melancholy. Accustomed to the blinding light of their ideas, they acknowledged its disturbing presence, but could not create an image of that brilliant black sun of which Nerval speaks. And if they did not succeed, it may be that no one in our modern world has been able to capture and explain the angel of melancholy. Kant was aware of its presence, explained the reasons why he was unable to see it, and never took a step towards it. Weber fearfully shut his eyes so as not to see it, only to stumble and fall unconscious in its arms. Benjamin thought he could glimpse the angel in the distance and went to greet it, but took his own life before he got there.

I should like to warn my readers, parodying the opening words of *Tristes Tropiques* by Claude Lévi-Strauss, that I hate exegeses and exhumations. And yet here I am proposing to dig up three abstruse thinkers, like someone exploring the ruins of a strange, exotic burial ground from some bygone era, littered with the primeval bones of a vanished tribe. To add to the sense of distance, I have chosen subjects whose languages are largely unfamiliar to me, from a part of Europe of which I know little. However, I have not chosen unknown examples, but very well-known and continually visited examples – real commonplaces, clichés that have often been commented on and analysed, and are part of the great traditions of European thought in the modern age: Enlightenment philosophy, scientific sociology and critical Marxism. Tristes topiques? Many believe these topics have been discussed so often they have withered, that they have been drawn on so often they have lost their meaning and have become dry: *Aufklärung, verstehenden Soziologie, kritische Theorie* . . . It seemed to me interesting to take the opposite approach to that of the traditional ethnologist. Driven by Rousseau's concerns, Lévi-Strauss travelled to primitive realms where he thought he would discover a sad, dying society – the Nambikwara – who to his eyes represented one of the poorest social and political organizations imaginable: a society so reduced to its simplest expression that it did not even have any institutions; as he said, the anthropologist found only men.[1] I, on the other hand, wished to travel to the heart of the modern world in search of a luminous state of rationality taken to its purest extreme, a state that possibly has never existed nor ever will, but about which we need to establish as precise an idea as possible if we are to understand our present situation. I went in search of it among the most brilliant thinkers who were part of complex societies and complicated war-torn situations. They themselves hid at the limits of extreme complexity, and when I reached them, I discovered that they were on the edge of an abyss.

In this book I present a brief exploration of the path bordering this abyss. I make no attempt to examine the long history of irrationality or of the ideas that emerge from irrational events. What interests me is to emphasize the importance of this corrosive, piercing humour that impregnates modernity. But here I prefer not to study melancholy in and of itself, but through an examination of the scars the illness left in Kant, Weber and Benjamin. I am interested in the sequels that this strange smell of death arising from modernity left in these three thinkers. This *Weltschmerz*, expressed in many ways, is not merely a critical shadow that accompanies modernity; I believe it is one of its most necessary and revealing expressions. It is the discontent that modern, enlightened man suffers when faced with the incoherent disorder he often has to confront, in both society and nature. Schiller, that restless writer who navigated between the Enlightenment and Romanticism, pointed out with great precision the strange links between melancholy and reason.

Sublime, melancholy feelings, Schiller believed, are not only produced by those things that the imagination cannot embrace: 'what is incomprehensible for the understanding, *confusion*, that can likewise serve as a representation of the supersensuous and supply the mind with an upward impulse.'[2] Faced with the radical otherness of the 'disordered chaos of appearances' and the 'wild incoherence of nature', mankind discovers the image of his freedom. This sense of strangeness shows itself to be completely independent, and this irrational chaos allows man to undertake the rational construction of a moral order. This makes it necessary to abandon the possibility of explaining nature, and to take this very incomprehensibility as the start of an explanation. In my view, these ideas are a demonstration of the strange ways in which irrationality combines with modern thought.

The extraordinary moral and rational order that Schiller discovers in mankind contrasts with the confusion and bewilderment he sees all around him: this is the measure of the distance separating man from the cosmos, a distance which underpins his proud independence. But the immensity of this distance has disturbed those who, sustained by a religious belief, are convinced, as Paul Claudel has it, that 'Creation is not a bazaar of heteroclite beings, haphazardly piled up.' In order to watch over and measure the boundaries, calls are usually made to those invisible mediators we know as angels, including those who have fallen and become demonic. One of the frequently quoted examples is the biblical angel of the Apocalypse, who measures the walls of the New Jerusalem with human measurements, to show that there is an affinity between celestial and human beings.[3] That is why I should like to place this book under the protection of the angels to whom Walter Benjamin was so attracted. For his part, Kant imagined that an angel could give him the choice of eternal life, whilst Weber talked of the devil who pulled the strings of his life. I should like to imagine these angels as strange beings . . . since they are neither benefactors nor incarnations of

God's enemy. As with Benjamin's angel of history, they are suffering beings who look on human destiny with sadness. Neither benign nor evil, they perform their rituals of mourning as an inescapable duty.

Melancholy as a Critique of Reason: Kant and Sublime Madness

Down melancholy's rapids
past the blank
woundmirror:
There the forty
stripped life-trees are rafted.

Paul Celan, *Breathcrystal*[1]

There are occasions when history offers us the fascinating spectacle of an ancient myth surprised, as one might say, at the precise moment when it takes root in the heads of the most rational of men. As if it were a live being lurking in the darkness rather than a phantasmagoria, myth seems to take advantage of the chance occurrences of daily life to slowly infiltrate its tentacles into the most hidden cerebral convolutions of a philosopher striding out majestically along the path of reason, illuminated by the solid principles that inhabit his individual consciousness. Something of the sort took place in the mid-eighteenth century in the calm Prussian city of Königsberg, where the philosopher Immanuel Kant lived. At the time he was hard at work as a modest *Privatdozent*, while attempting in the most disciplined way to bring order and coherence to an extremely complex world he knew of almost exclusively through books: although no longer young, he had only travelled a few kilometres out of his native city when the families employing him as a tutor went to stay in nearby villages. Having counted forty of his own 'life-trees', Kant was a sedentary fellow who did not like surprises. He once commented that if on his deathbed an angel offered him the choice between eternal life and total death, it would be very risky to choose an entirely unknown and unpredictable destiny, even if it were eternal.[2]

However, Kant's boring, orderly life was suddenly interrupted by the advent of a myth that might be said to have pursued the philosopher to eastern Prussia, not far from the Baltic Sea, and to have sidetracked him from his interests, which were concentrated on Newtonian physics, mathematics and theology. Let us remember that life in Königsberg was not exciting, and offered little intellectual stimulus. When Frederick the Great visited the city in 1739, he jokingly remarked that Königsberg was better suited to raising bears than to cultivating the sciences.[3] The city has been described as 'a backwater of complete calm, a place suited to reflection, without disturbances of any kind from what was agitating the world beyond it'.[4] It is possible therefore that the event which took Kant by surprise was an important stimulus that pushed him off-course and led him to the considerations that would make him famous many years later, when in 1781 he published his *Critique of Pure Reason*. The myth awaiting Kant, hidden in the woods close to Königsberg, was nothing less than an ancient legend establishing an odd, enigmatic link between reason and the madness of melancholy. Let us consider how the meeting between the professor and the myth took place.

Early in 1764, the local gazette published news of a remarkable, portentous event. A strange being had been found in the surrounding woods, a man of mature years who had apparently returned to a state of nature. This was a madcap adventurer by the name of Komarnicki, whom the gazette spoke of as a new Diogenes, a true spectacle of human nature, who 'sought to disguise the derisory, unseemly aspects of his way of life with a few vine leaves out of the Bible'. This madman had a lengthy beard, covered his naked body in goatskins, went around barefoot and bare-headed, and had arrived in Baumwalde accompanied by an eight-year-old boy and a flock of 46 goats, twenty sheep and fourteen cows. By the time the astonished inhabitants of Königsberg discovered him, he had already lost most of his flock, but always answered anyone who questioned him with a quotation from the Bible he carried in his hand. The locals christened him 'the madman of the goats'. It was said that the wild man's strange behaviour had been brought about by a stomach illness he had suffered seven years earlier, which had given him indigestion and gastric colic. These explanations were put forward by Johann Georg Hamann, the 'magus of the north', for the city gazette, the *Königsberger Gelehrte und Politische Zeitungen*, where this young, passionate irrationalist used the discovery to ensnare Kant in the nets of a problem that would challenge his scientific thought. Hamann, who had met Kant in 1756, used to call him the 'little magister', because of his small stature (Kant was 1.57 m (5 ft 2 in.) tall). Hamann concluded his commentaries by saying that everyone had gone to 'contemplate the adventurer and his boy. Also K[ant], whom many people asked for his opinion of this special phenomenon'.[5] Kant accepted the challenge.

In reality, the surprising arrival of this 'adventurer' offered the spectacle of a combination of two myths: the unhinged prophet was a disturbing example of the ancient legend according to which melancholy could converge with genius, or with the ability to see the future. At the same time, the little boy accompanying the prophet seemed to be a savage in a state of nature, a phenomenon that fascinated Enlightenment philosophers because it offered a rare opportunity to peer into the secrets of mankind's pure condition before he was contaminated by society and culture. Hamann laments that this opportunity had not been seized, since 'under the auspices of K[ant] they could have examined this boy, as few similar opportunities present themselves.' Unfortunately, the adventurer was allowed to move on, and he left the city's boundaries with the wild boy, never to be heard of again.

Kant, who had read Rousseau with admiration, was at first more interested in the 'little savage' than in the 'enthusiastic faun' – as he defines the madman possessed by the furies and divine inspiration. To an enlightened mind, the sectarians and lunatics who roamed Europe at that time seemed a less important phenomenon than the possibility of observing at first hand the 'raw nature' that was often concealed behind education. In the 'reasoning' Kant writes about the *kleine Wilde*, he points out that he is a perfect child for a sufficiently intelligent experimental moralist to test Rousseau's ideas, before rejecting them as beautiful fantasies. It is clear that Kant perceives and is troubled by the presence of the myth, and tries to skirt the danger by claiming that, far from being the object of laughter or mockery, it is necessary to channel the admiration inspired by the wild boy towards trying to explain this miracle, a portent which shows that the little one has learned to confront the harshness of life in nature with cheerful determination. Equally, his face displays none of the marks of that stupid timidity produced by servitude or forced education (except, Kant tells us, that some people have already corrupted the boy by teaching him to beg for money and sweets).

But in fact it was a different myth that really attracted Kant's attention. The same edition of the gazette that published (unsigned) the 'reasoning' about the wild child, together with Hamann's article, announced that in a future edition it would offer 'the first original investigation concerning the topic'. And in fact the next issue saw the publication, also anonymously, of one of Kant's most disturbing texts: 'Essay on the Maladies of the Head'. In this essay, an important addition to the famous 'Observations on the Feeling of the Beautiful and Sublime', also published in 1764, Kant is inspired not by the topic of the child of nature, but by the problem of the prophet adventurer's madness. He is disturbed by the similarities that might exist between the fantastic madness of the delirious prophet and the metaphysical passion of a professor obsessed by the ageing of the earth, the origin of the universe, the 1755 earthquake, the theory of the winds or of fire, syllogistic figures, and the demonstration of the existence of God. Could he himself be possessed by a madness similar to that of the prophet of the goats? Were philosophers also sick in the head?

The problem is troubling because Kant is convinced that maladies of the head have their origin in society, and so do not affect man in a natural state. The 'Essay' starts with a significant affirmation: 'The simplicity and frugality of nature only demands and forms common concepts and a clumsy sincerity in human beings.'[6] Kant seeks to name and classify the different forms of illness, which range from imbecility to madness, passing through foolishness. To do so, he examines the contrast between the alertness of the wild boy and the prophet Komarnicki's derangement:

> The human being in the state of nature can only be subject to a few follies and hardly any foolishness. His needs always keep him close to the experience and provide his sound understanding with such easy occupation that he hardly notices that he needs understanding for his actions.[7]

That is, natural man is too busy with the basic tasks of survival to fantasize or become delirious. The danger of madness lies in wait for civilized man, who has time to think. Savage brains only rarely show signs of illness. When this does happen, they become idiots or furious, but do not develop aberrations and fantasies, because man in a state of nature is free and can move around, which means they almost always enjoy good health. Although Kant appreciates Rousseau, it should be noted that from this time on, he marks his differences with the philosopher from Geneva. He thinks Rousseau adopts a synthetic approach that leads him to start from natural man. Kant on the other hand has an analytical approach, which begins from civilized man. And he points out: 'By nature we are not saints . . . the Arcadian pastoral and our gallant courtly life are equally *passé* and unnatural, although alluring Pleasure cannot be practised like a profession.'[8]

Kant believes that society has woven a thick veil that hides the secret judgements of head and heart, with the wise or modest excuse that we should spare ourselves the effort of using reasoning or uprightness. Although reason and virtue were becoming wide-spread and the arts were on the rise, the eagerness to extol them frees people from the need to actually cultivate and possess them, since when everything depends on art, subtle cunning appears much more useful, whereas sincere reactions become an obstacle: everyone thinks that trickery is better than stupidity. The obvious influence of Rousseau here completely justifies Kant's affirmation that: 'artificial constraint and the luxury of a civil constitution hatches punsters and subtle reasoners, occasionally however, also fools and swindlers.'[9] No mention is made of Komarnicki in the 'Essay on the Maladies of the Head', but it is plain that the Königsberg readers understood that Kant was referring to the 'enthusiastic faun' as a case of folly and madness. By not mentioning the prophet of the goats directly, the readers further understood the philosophy professor's mocking intention, extending his reflections to the rogues who gained pres-tige in civilized society. Doubtless Kant was thinking of the famous theosophist Emanuel Swedenborg, who had interested him greatly ever since he discovered that the Swedish mystic was apparently able to communicate with the spirit world. Swedenborg's prophetic visions could also be compared to the Leibniz-inspired speculations of the philosopher Christian Wolff. In 1766, only a few years after his observations on the maladies of the head, Kant published an enigmatic text on the visionary dreams of Swedenborg, which I will consider in due course. It is quite possible that Kant also had in mind Hamann himself as one of the outlandish products of civilized soci-ety, since he was someone who was not insensitive to the influence of Swedenborg, and who nourished his irrationality with a peculiar combination of impassioned energy and attacks of melancholy.[10]

Before considering the maladies of the head, Kant allows him-self a joke at the expense of those whom he calls the doctors of the understanding, who were fashionable at the time. These, he says, are the so-called logicians, who have made the important discovery that: 'the human head is actually a drum which only sounds because it is empty.'[11] Is he referring to the mind as a *tabula rasa*, as Locke had claimed? Are the causes of madness to be sought outside the head? Whatever the answer, Kant proceeds to an ingenious onomastic exercise concerning the 'frailties' of the head, naming and listing them rather than invoking the ancestral mishmash of cures.

ACCORDING TO KANT, there are two main categories of mental illness: a) those that do not negate free participation in the civil society of the affected individual; b) those where it is necessary to take measures to treat those subjects attacked by the evil. The first group are despised; the second, pitied.

Society disdains idiocy and foolishness, milder forms of the illness that are common in social life, but which can lead to the worst kinds of dementia. In order to comprehend these milder forms of madness, Kant takes as his starting point 'the drives of human nature'. When these drives are strong, they become passions. These drives are the 'moving forces of the will', and are more powerful than the understanding. This is why an irrational human being can possess understanding. For example, the force of amorous passion or ambition can turn reasonable people into irrational madmen. Other less strong tendencies or drives also produce foolishness, such as a mania to build, a love of paintings or a tireless search for books. Again, Kant makes reference to educated people, and doesn't spare wise men, whom he immediately makes fun of: we can only meet persons free of madness on the moon, where perhaps they can live without passions and in an infinitely rational state. But here in our sublunary society, passions affect reason. Insensitivity towards passions doubtless protects against folly, but does so because of stupidity, although the stupid are seen by ordinary people as wise. Foolishness [*Narrheit*] arises from two passions: arrogance and greed. These passions can be so powerful that they convert those who suffer from them into fools, to such an extent that they come to believe they already possess what they so greatly desire. Kant concludes with a racist touch typical of his time: trying to make a fool clever is like trying to wash a Moor. All the categories mentioned (dullards, buffoons and 'fantasts') are madmen who can live tranquilly in society, although any excessive increase in their numbers could lead one to fear they might take it into their heads to found a fifth monarchy . . .

Kant then turns to consider the serious kinds of mental illness, and it is here that he introduces fundamental elements of one of the oldest and most powerful myths about madness: melancholy. This notion was part of the complex structure of the theory of humours, whose influence was still strong in the mid-eighteenth century, and of which Kant was perfectly aware. Melancholy, in its hypochondriac form, appears to be the best explanation for the incredible fantasies, hallucinations and delusions that take possession of the disturbed mind. It is interesting to follow the manner in which Kant constructs a brief classificatory system around the old idea of melancholic madness, since, as we shall see, melancholy is to become one of the fundamental strands of his aesthetics.

His classification of illnesses of the mind establishes a division into two main groups. First', there are the illnesses of *impotency*, grouped under the general term of imbecility. The imbecile suffers from a great impotency of memory, reason and in general also of sensations. These illnesses are almost always incurable, because the disorder in the brain has turned it into a dead organ. Second', there are the types of illness that most interest Kant. These are the illnesses of *reversal*, or disturbances of the spirit. There are three main types:

- The reversal of empirical notions, which produces
  derangement (*Verrükung*).

- The disturbance of the faculty of judgement of immediate experiences, which produces *dementia* (*Wahnsinn*).
- The disturbance of reason to make more universal judgements, which causes *insanity* (*Wahnwitz*).

Considering this trilogy, a doubt immediately arises for me: is Kant suggesting that there are types of madness that are a kind of critique of reason? There is a curious and striking coincidence between the three kinds of reversal illness and the critical trilogy that Kant will go on to develop years later. In the deranged person who misinterprets empirical notions we can identify an eccentric critic of practical reason. Equally, the deranged sufferer who is incapable of judging the reality around him is akin to a proud but mistaken writer of a critique of reason. And finally, the insane person who upsets universal theoretical ideas could be a visionary absorbed in the preparation of a critical treatise on pure reason. Could Kant have discovered in the frailties of the head the rudiments of a transcendental method? Let us consider in turn each of these three versions of malign reversal as described by the philosopher.

The *deranged* person, who reverses the concepts of experience, usually suffers from hypochondria, an illness which travels erratically through the nervous tissue in different parts of the body, and which especially causes 'a melancholic haze around the seat of the soul'.[12] This reversal lies very close to normal life: the person affected is a dreamer who lives in a fantastic world peopled by chimeras, hallucinations and grotesque shapes such as we have all experienced. Kant defines this person as a 'fantast': someone who suffers from very painful internal phantasmagorias, believes he is beset by all manner of illnesses, grows anxious, gets ridiculous images in his brain that make him laugh at inopportune moments, is invaded by violent drives and seems very disturbed, although the illness is not deep-seated and either eases spontaneously or through medication. The most dangerous forms of reversal are those of the fanatics, whether they are visionaries or enthusiasts. A certain type of phantasmagoria produces feelings of extraordinary intensity: 'In this regard, the melancholic is a fantast with respect to life's ills.'[13] Similarly, many years later in his anthropology course of 1785, Kant described the typical existential discontent of the melancholic temperament as characterized by an intensity of feeling which lends everything a disproportionate importance and leads to excessive meditation. Kant concludes that the fact that 'everything seems to him so transcendental is the cause of his sadness'. He also observes that the melancholic with a high degree of understanding tends to be an enthusiast, whereas those with lesser understanding are usually fantasts.[14]

Unlike derangement, *dementia* – the second type of reversal – affects the understanding as well as the capacity to make judgements. This illness may be of three kinds: the person who feels they are being pursued or observed (nowadays we would call them paranoiacs), the arrogant person who believes everyone admires him, and the melancholic ('a gloomy person who is demented with respect to his sad or offensive conjectures').[15]

Finally, the most serious state is that of *insanity*, which completely disturbs reason and produces nonsensical judgements concerning universal concepts. However, there are cases in which correct judgements about experience still exist, where the faculty of sensation is intoxicated by all kinds of effects and novelties; even though the connections become blurred, this produces a very brilliant kind of dementia that can accompany great genius. In general, however, insanity reveals itself as raving madness or a vehement, noisy frenzy.

How can these frailties of the head be treated? Kant offers only a few suggestions, before going on to describe the causes that produce them. Those affected by *derangement* such as fantasts can be dealt with using rational arguments, since it is not their ability to understand that is affected, and so their illness can be eased. This is impossible with the *demented* and the *insane*, whose understanding is affected, so that any reasoning will simply provide them with fresh material to produce more absurdities: better to leave them be, as if we have not realized there was anything amiss in their understanding. Kant, who undoubtedly studied medicine at university, has consulted a medical journal and knows what the somatic causes of illnesses of the head are. He also knows, following the ancient medical interpretation, that the seat of madness lies in the digestive organs rather than in the brain. He employs the theory of humours to explain the illness of melancholy, whose gravest form is hypochondria, a pathological state which as its name indicates has its origin in the lower abdomen or spleen. Kant establishes a difference between the drives or passions that are the cause of less serious, more tolerable forms of mental illness (idiocy and foolishness) and the bodily, organic causes of the more serious expressions of madness. In these extreme cases, the cause has to be sought in the body, and not in arrogance, love, over-intense reflections or who knows what misuse of the soul's strengths, drives that produce ambiguous symptoms, love's fantastic raptures, fatuous attitudes or profound but vague ruminations.

At the end of his 'Essay', Kant introduces a surprising, bitter note of irony, which sees the philosopher himself in the role of the mentally disturbed: in fact, he has been preparing his readers for this switch throughout the work. To cure these sad ills it is necessary – he says – to see a physician, whom the philosopher can support by prescribing a diet for the mind, provided that he is not paid for it. The physicians, in return, could assist the philosopher who is trying (in vain) to cure his own madness. The frenzy of a learned writer could be cured by cathartic methods taken in large doses, as Jonathan Swift recommended when claiming that a bad poem is nothing more than a way of cleansing the brain, a method that allows the sick poet to get rid of 'many detrimental moistures' to relieve his condition. Kant suggests that for the philosopher the equivalent of writing a bad poem as a purge would be a 'miserable, brooding piece of writing'. And he ends with a disturbing, ambiguous suggestion that another way of purification could be sought: 'so that he would be thoroughly and quietly purged of the ill without disturbing the common weal through this'.[16] Could this be an unhinged invitation to suicide? An ironic invitation to shut oneself silently in the toilet? A melancholy praise of silence?

KANT NEVER OPTED for silence. Shortly before the arrival of the prophet of the goats inspired him to write his reflections on madness, the philosopher of Königsberg had purged his mind by writing a short treatise which, far from being miserable and brooding, is an extraordinarily rich, enchanting work: 'Observations on the Feeling of the Beautiful and Sublime', which was published in the same year that his text on the maladies of the head also appeared. Melancholy occupies a prominent position in his study of the beautiful and sublime, but in a different light: far from being a malign illness, Kant here sees it as a condition that stimulates the feeling of the sublime.[17] He makes it clear that the melancholic temperament sensitive to sublime things is not the gloomy illness that deprives individuals of the joy of living, a pathological state the melancholy can fall into when their sensations, if they become too intense, take them in the wrong direction. The melancholy character is not an illness, although it may degenerate into extravagances and delusions, leading to the kind of pathological state found in fantasts or cranks.

By associating melancholy with the sublime, Kant does something more than make a positive evaluation of the feelings associated with the black humour. In reality, the ideas on the sublime that Kant gathers and reworks contain, in a not always explicit manner, a melancholy texture that is full of subtleties. To Kant, the sublime is not seen as a continuation of the ancient Greek rhetorical tradition attributed to Longinus and rescued by Boileau in 1694, which referred to the extraordinary enthusiasm that certain passages from classical authors aroused in readers thanks to the employment of a refined, imaginative style. The idea of the sublime that Kant uses has been, one might say, fertilized by the melancholy feeling given to it by English writers from Milton to Edward Young culminating in the famous study by Edmund Burke, published in 1757: the *Philosophical Enquiry into the Origin of Our Ideas of the Sublime and Beautiful*, translated into German by Lessing in 1758. Burke describes the sublime in the following way:

> Whatever is fitted in any sort to excite the ideas of pain, and danger, that is to say, whatever is in any sort terrible, or is conversant about terrible objects, or operates in a manner analogous to terror, is a source of the sublime.[18]

This leads us to understand that the sublime goes beyond the purely rhetorical or aesthetic dimension to become a moral or anthropological category. Burke thought that fear and pain cause abnormal tension of the nerves, but that these horrendous nervous convulsions which produce sublime emotions occur more frequently in languid or inactive states. Taut and strengthened nerves, braced by exercise or work, help prevent the body from becoming immersed in that dangerous state of relaxation that exposes nervous tissue to sudden tensions. 'Melancholy, dejection, despair, and often self-murder,' says Burke, 'is the consequence of the gloomy view we take of things in this relaxed state of body'.[19] On the basis of these ideas, Burke explains that sublime feelings are produced by big, vast objects, by the infinite and the uniform, as well as by darkness and blackness. Kant follows in the same line and describes sublime feelings not merely in their relation to the grandeur of snowy peaks or furious storms, but also to situations and things linked to melancholy, such as night-time shadows, pensive thought, profound solitude and noble weariness. Time extended to the abyss of the past or the incalculable future also seems to him sublime, and he shudders with horror at the infinite panorama described by Albrecht von Haller, whom Kant regarded as the most sublime German poet, in his 'Unfinished Ode to Eternity'. Haller begins by invoking dark forests where no light can reach, where the plants look like tombs and the colours of death are spread everywhere, and ends by describing how his body senses that nothingness is approaching, and his nausea at this casts desperate shadows over the world. In a note to his poem, Haller himself warned that nobody should be angry because he talks of death as the end of being and of hope, and that he would have answered these objections if he had been able to complete his ode.[20]

Kant is very precise: melancholy is a 'gentle and noble sentiment' based on 'that dread which a restricted soul feels if, full of a great project, it sees the dangers that it has to withstand and has before its eyes the difficult but great triumph of self-overcoming'.[21] The melancholy temperament clearly encourages the feeling of the sublime, in contrast to the sanguine, whose dominant feeling is for the beautiful. Choleric individuals are insensitive to beauty, prone to dissembling, and their coldness or their vanity impedes them from perceiving the sublime. Kant simply ignores those of phlegmatic temperament, rejecting them because they are insensitive and lack any sublime or beautiful characteristics.[22] In the pyramid of values Kant constructs, melancholy is plainly at the summit, since in addition to being a temperament capable of perceiving the charms of beauty, it surrenders above all to the powerful enchantments of the sublime without abandoning high principles, detests lies and pretence, extols friendship, aspires to freedom, rejects all abject submission, becomes a stern judge of itself and others, and often feels as weary with itself as with the world around it. The sublime things that the melancholic can perceive constitute a heterogeneous collection that was obvious to the eyes of an eighteenth-century philosopher even if today they may appear strange or eccentric: I have already mentioned lofty mountain peaks, eternity and night, but Kant also associates the sublime with Milton's kingdom of hell, the tall oaks in sacred groves, the lonely Moon, the vast desert of Shamo in Tartary, the pyramids of Egypt, the basilica of St Peter's, understanding, boldness, Young's poetry, friendship, tragedy, war, Achilles' wrath, the colour black and black eyes, advanced age, true virtue, the masculine, profound intelligence, the English, Spaniards and Germans, but also Arabs and the noble savages of North America, etc., etc. The list of everything associated with the beautiful would be equally heteroclite, since in reality Kant is writing a treatise on the science of customs rather than an essay on aesthetics: everything grouped together under the notion of the sublime is coherent when considered from a moral perspective attempting to classify, by means of the theory of humours, his views about honour, vice, kindliness, dignity, nobility, envy, greed, generosity, ostentation and other concepts related to patterns of behaviour.

The myth of melancholy was deeply imbued in the cultural atmosphere by which Kant was surrounded. He praises it as a dangerous temperament that is nonetheless capable of leading one to the enjoyment of the most sublime feelings. The philosopher of Königsberg therefore already possessed a conceptual net capable of ensnaring the melancholy prophet who appeared in Baumwalde in January 1764. The problem is that the melancholy represented by the strange wild visionary revealed itself in its most grotesque and extravagant form as an illness rather than as a way towards the enjoyment of the sublime. However, in both cases melancholy was a feeling that escaped reason and led to those dark, grandiose spaces where the philosopher's eyes are blind, incapable of understanding the mysteries of pleasure and horror. This is why at the start of his essay on the beautiful and sublime,

Kant signals that he will use rather the eyes of an observer than those of the philosopher. He could have exclaimed, like Milton in 'Il Penseroso':

> Hail, divinest Melancholy!
> Whose Saintly visage is too bright
> To hit the sense of human sight;
> And therefore to our weaker view,
> O'er-laid with black, staid Wisdom's hue.[23]

Kant's enthusiasm for melancholy did not blind him to the hidden threats lurking in the darkness of sublime night. These involve the strange varieties melancholy can degenerate into if it descends to the most abject imperfection. The extravagant praise for deeds is typical of fantasts, those visionaries who take the feeling of the sublime and beautiful beyond the normal, which is why – according to Kant – they are usually classified as romantic experiences.[24] This anti-natural exacerbation of the sublime produces various types of madness, arrogance, insanity and grotesque or extravagant behaviour, such as the devotion of hermits to tombs, the cult of the holy bones of martyrs or the saintly defecations of the great Lama of Tibet. Melancholy may also accompany a terrifying perception of the sublime, as in the case of profound solitude, which Kant illustrates with an example taken from a magazine in Bremen, describing the horrible dream of a rich miser, very religious but not inclined to feel any love for his fellow man, who is cast into an abyss of solitude: 'As I approached the most extreme limit of nature, I noticed that the shadows of the boundless void sank into the abyss before me. A fearful realm of eternal silence, solitude and darkness!'[25] Faced with horrors such as these, Kant could have remembered another of Milton's poems, 'L'Allegro', in which he outlines the dangers of melancholy:

Hence, loathèd Melancholy,
Of Cerberus and blackest Midnight born,
In Stygian cave forlorn
'Mongst horrid shapes, and shrieks,
and sights unholy!

It is well known that Kant was forever obsessed by boundaries, and that even the great revolution in his thought represented by his *Critique of Pure Reason* has its origins in a lengthy reflection on the frontiers between feelings and reason, and in a concern for defining the limits of knowledge. In his discussion of the beautiful and the sublime he establishes, from the very first sentence in the essay, that feelings do not chiefly depend on 'external things' but on the feelings of each individual, which are rooted deep in the temperaments and humours. Over time, these 'external things' will come to be conceived by Kant as the famous *ding an sich*, the *noumenon* or impenetrable 'thing in itself' that reason cannot know, although it can think of it as a frontier concept, as Ernst Cassirer explains, which serves to delimit our sensibility?[26]

At times it seems as if Kant is interested in madness because, in some strange way, the sick mind can go beyond the frontier of sensitivity and phenomena, beyond which a terrible darkness exists. Furthermore, we should remember that, as one of his biographers has pointed out, Kant considered himself to have a melancholy temperament, and that his reflections on this score are to a certain extent a self-portrait.[27] What would happen – Kant may have asked himself – if someone crossed the prohibited border and penetrated the *noumenon*? Would he lose his reason as he moved away from the *phaenomenon*? Doubtless, this experience could signify a plunge into what is thinkable but not knowable by the senses, and therefore a mind that succeeded in crossing the threshold, when it understood life's lack of meaning, could become sick, unbalanced or sink into madness since apparently the sick person was trying to go beyond the limits of knowledge and enter a dark region filled with visions and phantasmagoria of uncertain origin. Noble melancholy could be an alternative way of *feeling* the vertigo experienced when faced with the mouth of the black abyss, in an unhealthy attempt to penetrate the impenetrable. But if for some reason human beings attempt to pierce nature in a wish to go beyond the senses without reason having already established its own intentions, they may reach a dark, mysterious world where everything is complicated, jumbled and unbalanced.

TWO YEARS AFTER Kant's reflections on the maladies of the head and sublime melancholy appeared, he undertook another disturbing journey into the dark, mythical territory that is so attractive to madmen and visionaries. 'The realm of shadows', says Kant in 1766, 'is the paradise of fantastical visionaries. Here they find a country without frontiers which they can cultivate at their pleasure. Hypochondriacal exhalations, old wives' tales and monastery miracles do not leave them short of building materials to construct it.'[28] These are the opening lines of *Dreams of a Spirit-seer Elucidated by Dreams of Metaphysics*, in which melancholy appears as hypochondria and is represented by the madness of the famous Swedish mystic Emanuel Swedenborg.

Kant was never interested in Swedenborg's theology, which he saw as a simple 'madness of reason' (*Wahnsinn*, or dementia) since illusory experiences seem to him much more revealing than the deliberations of a mistaken reasoning.[29] Kant has the same opinion of those who dream: there are 'dreamers of reason', like Christian Wolff and Christian August Crusius, who build mental worlds in the air that are full of contradictions and bear little relation to our experiences; but there are also 'dreamers of feeling', who are much more interesting since they claim to communicate with spirits, say they have seen apparitions or chimeras and assert that they have visited the world of ghosts.[30] This explains why Kant took such a great interest in investigating the feats of Swedenborg, someone supposedly endowed with an extraordinary capacity for communicating with souls and spirits that live separated from their bodies. Kant also read very carefully the eight volumes of his *Arcana Coelestia*, where the Swedish mystic explains among many other things that there exists a world of spirits with which it is possible to enter into contact. In a famous letter to Charlotte von Knobloch, possibly written in 1763, Kant explains the results of his enquiries into Swedenborg's adventures in the mysterious realm of invisible spirits and the souls of the dead. There are two proofs that the Swedish theologian communicated with the souls of the dead: the first example is the story of the deceased Dutch ambassador in Stockholm who indicated to him the exact spot where a document could be found that his widow needed to prove she had paid off a large debt. The second case, which Kant saw as very convincing, concerns a story according to which the spirits informed Swedenborg, who was in Gothenburg, about a fire which at that very moment was spreading through the streets of Stockholm; the confirmation of this news apparently only arrived two days later.[31] While Kant quotes these examples in *Dreams of a Spirit-seer Elucidated by Dreams of Metaphysics*, they are here regarded as negligible stories that only interest him in comparison to metaphysical speculation, which also seems to him a cock-and-bull story. However, the fact is that Kant was fascinated by Swedenborg the visionary almost as much, if not more, than the prophet Komarnicki: he drew lessons about what he called the 'realm of shadows' from both men.

More than as a prophet or theologian, Kant treats Swedenborg as a sick person who has fantastic dreams, suffers from a nervous imbalance, and has a malformation of some of his brain organs. This is a phenomenon explained by means of a kind of cerebral optics, in which a malformation means that the directional lines place the imaginary focus outside the head, creating fantasy images that affect the senses by creating illusions, even though they do not touch the understanding. This being the case, the profound metaphysical considerations about the existence of a world of bodiless spirits are of little use when it comes to understanding the deceptions of a poetizing reason and the inferences made by visionaries, who, rather than being citizens of this other world, this great beyond, are subjects who should be sent to the clinic. However, Kant does admit that he was naive enough to allow himself to undertake an investigation into Swedenborg's ghosts. In the letter to Charlotte von Knobloch, Kant defines the Swedish mystic as an erudite, wise man who is both friendly and frank, and to whom he has written to find out more about his spiritual feats. By contrast, in *Dreams of a Spirit-seer Elucidated by Dreams of Metaphysics* he presents him as 'a certain Mister Schwedenberg [sic], 'of independent position' living in Stockholm off his considerable fortune. Not only does he misspell his name, but he describes him as an 'arch-visionary', even though he admits he has spent seven pounds sterling on buying his books and allowed himself to be taken in for a while.[32] The acidly ironic tone of Kant's text still surprises today's readers, who wonder for what reasons the Königsberg professor could have allowed himself to be deceived by the 'mystery' of Swedenborg's visions. Be that as it may, Kant's lucid and entertaining text could perhaps have been his small revenge for having been seduced by the trickery of false prophets.

However, despite the irony, Kant also raises the concern that troubles him: the phantasmagoria of the false prophet are surprisingly similar to his own philosophical chimera. The eight volumes *in quarto* of the *Arcana Coelestia* do not contain so much as a drop of reason, and yet in them there is an extraordinary coincidence 'with what the finest subtlety of reason may discover', similar to that of those who discover in chance formations – such as veins in marble, frozen windowpanes or stalagmites – images of the Holy Family or the number of the Beast. Swedenborg claims to have discovered a world of immaterial beings who form a great society under the appearance of a Greatest Man, a vast spiritual presence that for Kant is nothing more than a 'monstrous and gigantic fantasy'.[33] But to reflect on this dark world is not a frivolous occupation; it serves to put metaphysics to the test, insofar as the task of this science is to employ reason to discover the hidden properties of things. Faced with the fantasy of the Greatest Man, metaphysics becomes the science of the limits of human reason, because it is plain that when one crosses certain boundaries – as the mad do – one enters a strange region where all exploration is useless, since an investigation that aims to collect its data in this other world, the dark realm where there are no sensations, is doomed to failure.

However, to prove the sterility of a journey to the world of immaterial beings, Kant paradoxically attempts to uncover the laws governing that strange *mundus intelligibilis* (composed of immaterial substances). Of course, this is an ironic explanation of specific laws: Kant takes advantage of the fusion of Aristotelian theories with Galenist medical traditions, with regard to the behaviour of that vital spirit known as the *pneuma*, an extraordinary, subtle substance formed by vapours or animal exhalations that supposedly stimulate the movements of the soul. In Kant's day there still flourished a branch of philosophical and theological studies called pneumatology, which sought to elaborate a theory of spiritual beings. The spirit world was apparently governed by *pneumatic* laws, which would explain the flow of spiritual substances and the movement of winds and vapours in the disposition of moral strengths and wills. These pneumatic laws, which explain the interaction between bodies and souls, continue to operate in spirits even after the death of their bodies.

We should remember that Kant began his reflections on Swedenborg's dreams with an allusion to hypochondriac exhalations, which together with old wives' tales and monastery miracles helped construct the strange realm of the shades. According to

Galenist tradition, hypochondriac vapours, the product of the dangerous combustion of humours in the lower abdomen or spleen, expanded by means of pneumatic processes to the heart and head, producing melancholy, madness and mania. I have already pointed out how, in his study of the maladies of the head, Kant directly refers to the theory according to which madness has its origin in the digestive tract, and can be cured by a purge of the humours, since their inflammation produces exhalations and winds whose excess has to be expelled by means of cathartic remedies. Kant takes the idea that the effort of writing is equivalent to a purge from a very amusing text frequently attributed to Swift which is, it must be stressed, a parody of the sublime sentiments found in the cultivation of the art of poetry. Swift claims that it would be not only unjust but cruel to prohibit non-sublime forms of writing, since in reality poetry is a natural or unhealthy secretion of the brain, whose flow it is unwise to stop. Every adult has experienced some kind of poetic evacuation which has contributed to his health. 'I have known a man,' says Swift, 'thoughtful, melancholy, and raving for divers days, but forthwith grow wonderfully easy, lightsome and cheerful, upon a discharge of peccant humour, in exceeding purulent metre.'[34] Kant extended Swift's irony to his reflections on Swedenborg, but in this case used as a reference the jokes he found in *Hudibras*, Samuel Butler's great comic poem, which had just been published in German in 1765. Kant suggests that the fantastic visionaries, the followers of the spirit world – who in other ages were burned – could now be merely purged, and that there was no need to turn to metaphysics to understand the deceptions practised by the Swedish prophet, but rather to consider the verses of the English comic writer, who explained how the pneumatic laws of corporal winds allowed one to grasp that 'if a hypochondriacal wind should rage in the guts, what matters is the direction it takes: if downwards, the result is a f---; if upwards, an apparition or an heavenly inspiration.'[35]

IN 1766 KANT closed the door to metaphysics in an ironic, anti-sublime way so that the winds of madness or the dreams of visionaries could not enter. From this moment on Kant appears to lose interest in the mythical realm of shades and spirits, and instead devotes himself to constructing the immense critical system which, like a vast wall, will mark out with great precision the limits of knowledge and the boundaries between feelings and reason.[36] The two great fortresses that Kant builds in these years – the *Critique of Pure Reason* and the *Critique of Practical Reason* – distance the philosopher from the tempting realms of madness and sublime darkness. At around the same time, Kant also closed the doors to eroticism and love for women. He apparently was in love on two occasions only, but ended up rejecting matrimony to devote himself entirely to his work. Still extant is a letter from Maria Charlotta Jacobi, an extremely beautiful woman trapped in an unfortunate marriage that was eventually dissolved, in which she indirectly proposes an intimate relation to Kant. We do not know whether he resisted the lady's charms, but he never consented to abandoning bachelorhood. He once commented that when he had needed a woman he was in no position to maintain her, and by the time he was earning enough he no longer needed female company.[37] As far as is known, Kant never had sexual relations with a woman. Did the lack of love contribute to his melancholy? However that may be, his aversion towards dreams and madness were akin to his rejection of eroticism.

When the philosopher Moses Mendelssohn expressed surprise that Kant had written about Swedenborg's visions, Kant explained that he had approached the topic out of a wish not to be taken in by deception – which could corrupt his character – even though he admits he thinks 'many things that I shall never have the courage to say, [but] I shall never say anything I do not believe.'[38] Further on in the same letter he says that healthy, clear understanding only requires an *Organon* to understand things, whereas 'the illusory knowledge of a corrupted mind first has need of a *Catarticon*.' Is Kant implying that his text on prophetic madness and the dark realm of the spirits was a purge or catharsis of his own mind? Is he suggesting that his ironic comments on the realm of spiritual shades refer to things he does not have the courage to reveal? However that may be, Kant stubbornly devoted himself to raising his immense critical *Organon*: to building the solid architecture of the theoretical and methodological principles that direct the accumulation of knowledge, and to defining the kinds of sensibility, understanding and reason that *a priori* experience permits. Kant later used the concept of *Catarticon* to refer to that part of logic which allows us to see through deception and to describe the psychological or empirical conditions that affect understanding. In *Dreams of a Spirit-seer Elucidated by Dreams of Metaphysics* Kant had already pointed out that, when considering the possible existence of a world of souls and spirits without bodies, the balance of understanding was tilted by the weight of hope in future survival, by the 'foolish hope that in some way or other we continue to exist after death'. Kant admits that in this case his intellectual balance is at fault and confesses that this is 'the only inexactitude I am unable to suppress and which, in fact, I have no wish to suppress'.[39] This was the catharsis he needed to help him survive the rigours of a reason that excluded hope.

A quarter of a century after the prophets Komarnicki and Swedenborg – the wild madman and the civilized visionary – had inspired Kant's reflections on the foolish and noble forms of melancholy, our philosopher once again opened the door to the sublime. On the threshold of old age, Kant finds that his critical system is not complete, and feels the need to extend its coherence beyond the boundaries of consciousness and probe the supersensible spaces of the imagination and aesthetic pleasure. He does this in the *Critique of Judgement* (1790), where he devotes a considerable part to the 'analytic of the sublime' in what is undoubtedly the most intense and beautiful section of the book. For Kant – who draws his inspiration from Burke – the feeling of the sublime is still a sensation of awe and horror faced with the spectacle of lofty mountains, unleashed natural forces, the depths of the abyss, and 'solitudes'.[40] In this instance, however, Kant no longer privileges the melancholic temperament as the best starting point from which to experience the sublime. Now, melancholy is substituted by an ethical consideration: a faculty for judging the supersensible that comes from a moral feeling. For Kant, who did not understand a great deal about art, it is an aesthetic judgement which, thanks to its moral strength, allows one to go beyond the limits of consciousness to contemplate those natural objects that produce sublime emotions. The gaze of the aesthete-philosopher once again penetrates the world beyond consciousness, but on this occasion it is not visionaries or melancholics who act as guide, but moral sentiments. It remains true that the states of mind that stimulate the faculty of overstepping boundaries to immerse oneself in sublime feelings still maintain some kind of relationship with the myth of melancholy madness: submission, prostration, the sense of impotence, solitude, sadness and fear. The imagination feels it has no limits and can abolish the boundaries of consciousness to peer into the infinite abyss. Kant maintains that enthusiasm is sublime when it lends the spirit a more powerful and lasting impulse than sensorial representations, even though he also recognizes that it may lead to the extravagance of visionaries or dreamers and to madness, whether these are passing accidents that a healthy understanding encounters, or illnesses that unbalance it.

The capacity to judge the sublime is produced by a sudden blockage of the vital forces, followed by their powerful release, when the spirit is successively attracted and repulsed by the object producing the emotion. We might think of an orgasm, and Kant immediately warns the reader that this is a negative pleasure. The object that awakens the sublime emotion is always part of nature, and artistic objects can only provoke it by indirect means. Certain natural spectacles (the vast ocean, for example) arouse sublime aesthetic emotions not because they lead us to the study of the objective principles controlling them, but on the contrary because they are a wild vision of disorder and desolation. These images, which would appear to refer to erotic or deluded experiences, are alluded to by Kant to analyse the presence within us of a supersensible faculty that allows the imagination to approach the infinite: 'the sublime is . . . the mere capacity of thinking which evidences a faculty of mind transcending every standard of sense.'[41] As a consequence, the objects of nature are not in themselves sublime, only the spiritual disposition of the spirit representing them.

Of course, the ability to 'think the infinite' goes beyond the boundaries of consciousness. Since the infinite grandeur and dimensions of nature, in their absolute totality, are inconceivable, the spirit turns to a supersensible substratum which consists precisely in the aesthetic ability to judge the sublime. Kant wishes to go beyond the boundaries usually crossed by visionaries, prophets or the melancholy mad, but without losing reason. That is the challenge he faces. The same challenge as that faced by Ulysses when he decided to listen to the sirens' song without risking his life. Kant wants to feel the vertigo when confronting the abyss. That abyss opens up at the spot where the imagination admits its impotence and limits, faced with an object it cannot conceive. This impotence produces an unpleasant vertigo, paradoxically accompanied by the pleasure of a reason that is able to guide the fall over the precipice.

The cosmos's infinite abyss is threatening and provokes horror. But fear paralyses the ability to judge, and therefore blocks the feeling of the sublime. On the contrary, what we seek is to penetrate the insensible and meaningless world – indifferent to our presence – to endow it with meaning. The danger posed by ravines, storm clouds, erupting volcanoes, hurricanes, tempests at sea and powerful waterfalls can only arouse a sublime feeling as long as – like Ulysses tied to his mast – we ourselves are secure. The fact that the danger is not real, says Kant, does not imply that the sublime character of our intellectual faculty is also unreal. It is sublime because it reveals in the spirit of man a superiority and independence with regard to nature, a capacity to formulate laws *a priori* – and these are precisely the bonds that tie anyone navigating the stormy waters of the sublime to the secure mast of sound judgement. And, paradoxically, it is these bonds that define the fundamental freedom of human beings.

As Isaiah Berlin has pointed out, Kant was driven mad by the nature of things, whereas for Rousseau, madness was caused entirely by ill will.[42] Kant was afraid that the natural order and laws would impose themselves on his free will. He obsessively opposed any force – human, natural or divine – that limited or determined man's autonomy. This obsession with freedom made him one of the precursors of Romanticism, despite the fact that he detested all of its manifestations. But he loathed them precisely because he found them extraordinarily seductive, as we have seen in his fascination with extravagances, the spirit world, mystical fantasies, mental disorder taken to wild extremes, oneiric visions, hope in the great beyond and sublime melancholy. These were all topics about which the Romantics were passionate. They exalted the existence of a mysterious, dark world where enlightened reason could not enter, inhabited by primeval freedom, death, illnesses, the *Belle Dame sans merci*, melancholy, the exuberance of nature and primordial chaos. The explanation for Kant's fascination with the dark side of reality lies in the fact that he wishes to penetrate into the nature of things with the same freedom as a madman who strolls naked along the street, defining the future according to his own desires, conversing with phantoms, terrorizing or enthusing, overturning orders and hierarchies. However, unlike a madman, the rational being is guided by moral principles, even if these merge in an essential freedom that occasionally can be confused with the untethered madness of disturbed and extravagant minds. The threshold Kant seeks to cross takes him to a strange dimension of the nature of things: a mathematical, dynamic grandeur that sustains sublime feelings. It is easy nowadays to recognize the mythical nature of the sublime, but in Kant's day it was a dimension widely accepted as a topic for philosophic enquiry, in both its physiological and ethical expressions, with the same conviction as Newton's physics allowed one to understand the cosmos. Kant in fact was captivated by the great myth of the sublime, and was caught in its nets. The powerful beam of his thought did not dispel the shadows of the myth; on the contrary, it served to emphasize its presence.

It has been said that Kant was incapable of seeing that his thought depended on the myth. Moreover, as Milton Scarborough points out, he was possibly not even aware that the transcendental ego was an expression of the craftsman demiurge of the Platonic myth of *Timaeus*.[43] However that may be, I am convinced that the trinity composed of melancholy, the infinite and the sublime is a creation of mythical thinking, even as defined by Cassirer, the great twentieth-century neo-Kantian philosopher. The three aspects of the myth allow us to define a transcendental inner flow whose force – melancholy madness – is capable of leading us beyond 'sensible' limits to contemplate immortality or eternity, and then, thanks to a feeling of sublime morality, allow us a heroic return to normal life. This is not the ecstatic journey of a modern Prussian shaman (nothing could be further from Kant's petit-bourgeois common sense) but the expression of a mythical thought caught in the powerful nets of enlightened rationalism. However, Kant's critical fortress did not silence the myth: its echoes were perceived soon afterwards by the Romantics, who spoke of this painful and nostalgic wish to engender the infinite out of the finite, as Friedrich Creuzer said. He was referring to the power of those symbols that represent the incongruence between eternal essence and its limited representation, which myths then express in a coded manner.[44] Many years later, Rudolf Otto also revisited what he called 'the dark content of the idea *a priori*' mooted by Kant, to refer to the *mysterium tremendum* of the sacred and numinous.[45] Kant's sublime melancholy is in reality the space reserved for the mythical and the sacred, except that here the circle of the sacred is depicted in profane colours, and the irrational is expressed in a non-religious form, in an enlightened, philosophical manner. Cassirer himself implicitly accepts this fact when he asserts that all theories attempt to locate the origin of the mythical in certain psychic states or experiences, chiefly in oneiric phenomena or in the contemplation of natural occurrences, such as astronomical events or spectacular meteorological processes (tempests, flashes of lightning or thunder). Although Cassirer is referring to primitive peoples, we cannot help but think of Kant's sublime awe at the mysteries of nature.[46] 'My mother,' Kant told Jachmann, 'often took me out of the city and had me admire the marvels of creation. She was the one who gave me the first idea of the good, and her influence on me lasts to this day.'[47]

IN THE SUMMER of 1792, Kant writes a letter to Prince Alexandr von Beloselsky which, in addition to being interesting as it offers a synthesis of his entire critical system, allows us to understand the position of madness in the overall framework of his thought. Kant explains that there are two great areas of innate representation: *thought* and *perception*. Thought itself contains three spheres: the first is *understanding*, the second is *judgement* and the third is *reason*. Understanding is the faculty for constructing concepts; judgement is the faculty for applying those concepts concretely; and reason is the faculty for deducing the particular from the universal, in agreement with principles. When these three faculties are integrated into a system – which is what Kant did in his three *Critiques* – we are in the sphere of philosophy. On the other hand, when the three faculties are integrated in intuition (and especially its quintessential component, the originality represented by imagination) they become part of the sphere of genius. Kant points out that imagination is a power that does not follow the rules obediently, but claims to create itself, as is the case in the arts. Kant concludes his letter with a warning that not only shows he has not forgotten madness, but that he attributes great importance to it:

> In this manner I can discover five spheres. If, in the end, imagination annihilates itself by capricious activity, it turns into common foolishness or into nervous disorder; when imagination escapes the rule of reason and even tries to subjugate it, man leaves the estate (the sphere) of mankind and descends into the sphere of madness and phantoms.[48]

Madness and phantasmagorias occur when the imagination, in a sublime impulse similar to the one driving artists on, transgresses the sphere of genius and strays into a dangerous dimension.

Melancholy madness would therefore be located in a disturbing sixth sphere, one that contains a dark underworld where the imagination completely dominates reason. At this point it is worthwhile remembering the importance Kant lent to the 'dark representations', as he termed everything that human beings are unconscious of: 'only a few places on the vast map of our mind are illuminated', he wrote in his *Anthropology from a Pragmatic Point of View*.[49] Kant published this maxim as an old man, in 1798, the date of publication of one of his most fascinating yet underrated texts.[50] The *Anthropology from a Practical Point of View* is a captivating work that aims, in a succinct summary, to set out the rules of conduct that arise from his critical philosophy. In so doing, Kant opens up his system to the culture and customs in which he was immersed, and allows daily life to make an ingenious incursion into his work. This immersion in the mores and commonplaces of his time could be what has troubled many commentators, because it is true that the *Anthropology* is full of advice, prudent warnings and opinions on a wide range of topics, from courtesy, boredom and fainting fits to monsters, prophecies, dreams, weeping or vengeance. However, it is not a disorganized book: on the contrary, thanks to a logical, coherent structure, it allows many of the day-to-day concerns that preoccupied his contemporaries to find their place and explanation: fashion, luxury, passions, cowardice, the nature of the sexes, physiognomy, races and the natural and wild state of humanity. Of course, Kant's major themes occupy most of the *Anthropology*: imagination, knowledge, pleasure and understanding.

In the *Critique of Pure Reason* Kant had already pointed out that the territory of pure understanding is an island isolated by nature within unchanging boundaries; this island of truth is surrounded by a huge, stormy ocean inhabited by illusions: a dark realm which the light of truth is unable to penetrate. This area of dark figures is, according to Kant, the greatest of all in man. As an example, he cites sexual love, which illustrates the close relationship of man with other animals, and in which the imagination likes 'to stroll in darkness'. The theme of melancholic or hypochondriac madness – one which borders on the dark side of mankind – is treated in his *Anthropology from a Practical Point of View* in a definitely pragmatic and even colloquial and popular manner. Here he divides the sickness of the soul, seen as defects in the faculty of knowledge, into two main categories: the 'illness of the crickets' and mental derangement. Strictly speaking, the former is hypochondria, and its popular name comes, as Kant explains, from the analogy with the chirping noise of a cricket in the silence of the night.[51] We cannot help but recall that the philosopher himself could not bear the noise, not of a cricket but of a neighbour's cock, whose crowing kept interrupting his meditations: when the neighbour refused to sell him the bird at any price to be sacrificed on the altar of silence, Kant simply moved house.[52] 'The hypochondriac is a chaser of crickets (fantast) of the most lamentable sort,' Kant writes, 'obstinate, unable to be talked out of his imaginings', obsessed by non-existent physical diseases, or ones brought on by flatulence that creates obsessive concerns.[53] The hypochondriac is close to madness because of his fits or sudden mood swings, the outbursts that can lead him to suicide, his fear of death and the illusions he has of 'profound thought' that produces a type of melancholy (*Tiefsinnigkeit*). The 'cricket hunter' whose imagination oversteps the laws of experience is a *fantast* who dreams while awake; and if he does so while influenced by emotion, he becomes an *enthusiast*. Kant also speaks of a 'worm', which he defines as a melancholy confusion of internal sense.

The second kind of sickness of the soul consists of mental derangement, or as is commonly said, madness. The *Anthropology* offers a slightly different classification in this respect from the one Kant employed in his essay on the maladies of the head. He now divides madness into two groups: first, those kinds that disturb the representation of the senses, such as *amencia* and *demencia*; secondly, those that upset judgement and reason, like *insania* and *vesania*. In addition, Kant adds (without any great explanation) a tripartite division that typifies the tumultuous, methodological and systematic forms of madness. It is likely that this classification was influenced by a visit Kant made to the Königsberg lunatic asylum, which his university colleague Johann Heinrich Metzger described in the following way:

> On the lowest floor there are four or five garrets or damp chambers in which approximately 200 madmen or idiots are packed in like sardines in a barrel; the violent ones are kept in wretched, very narrow wooden cells like pigsties, above in the cells and below in the garrets, all of them as close to each other as possible . . . I never saw that any of

these cells had been ventilated, or that they had been cleaned in any way; still less that the mad had been washed: they were left to roll around in their own excrement in the narrow confines of this tip.[54]

By contrast, the mad are very well classified and separated in Kant's mind. *Amencia* is a tumultuous form of madness shown by the disjointed nature of its representations: the asylums, he says, are full of talkative women affected by this disturbance. *Demencia* has a methodical character, and is shown by fictitious perceptions like those of people who see themselves surrounded by enemies pursuing them: they are incurable. *Insania* is also methodical, but in a fragmented way, and is characterized by the fact that the sick person invents absurd, illogical things: this kind of lunatic is also incurable, Kant says, 'because, like poetry in general, he is creative and entertaining by means of diversity'.[55] When later on he refers to the character of genius, he admits that it is not completely subject to rules, but that if it frees itself completely from them it can end up as a raving madness that may be original but is not genius. In another passage, Kant affirms that *demencia* with emotion produces a frenzy that is often original and when it occurs in an involuntary way is close to genius, as in the case of poetic rapture.[56] It is important to note that, for Kant, the sublime is not part of taste, but is a feeling linked to emotion.[57] Finally we have *vesania*, a systematic madness that disturbs reason and leads those suffering from it to believe they can unveil the supersensible forces of nature, discover how to square the circle or comprehend the mystery of the Trinity. Here, Kant points out the dangers of provoking an artificial dementia in oneself by the use of wolfsbane, opium or camphor to experiment with the soul and sicken it so as to observe it and discover its nature.

Towards the end of his life, as his *Anthropology* shows, Kant remains deeply concerned with the boundaries that madness imposes on reason. His investigation of the frontiers bordering the abyss, thanks to the experiences of the sublime and genius, is without doubt a kind of logical necessity of his critical system, because it permits him to point out or to point to the absolute Idea, the indeterminate, the limitless and the formless. The problem, as Jean-François Lyotard has expressed it, consists in finding a way to present the absolute by aesthetic means, means which always depend on the form.[58] How can one present the formless by means of forms? The solution lies in the experience of the sublime. We could add that the melancholic feeling of the sublime is also an experience of the sacred, a religious emotion and an expression of our existential anguish faced with death, the formless and the unnameable. In Lyotard's view, it could be added that Kant's sublime melancholy discovers modern and even post-modern aesthetic expressions insofar as they open the way to a nostalgia for the unattainable totality, and insist on emphasizing the fact that the unpresentable exists.[59] In modern art there appears to be a Kantian obsession with the impotence of the faculty of presentation: the *Darstellungsvermögen* that the nineteenth-century translators of Kant into Spanish called the *facultad de exhibición*, a troubling expression which I like that alludes to the spectacular struggle of the imagination against reason.[60] This struggle posits an imagination that feels a violent repulsion at being unable to pursue reason, which for its part is attracted to those delightful and unreachable spaces of infinite, absolute and total ideas.

Exhibition contrasts with inhibition, and also with prohibition: if the imagination breaks loose and crosses the boundary following a reason that is searching for the absolute, it will collapse into madness. It must inhibit its mad flight so that, at the extreme limit, it exhibits a spectacle of sublime melancholy, as a fleeting glimpse of that which has no form or limit. This is why Kant sees as admirable the iconophobia of the ancient Jews, who forbade the creation of images of the absolute divinity:

Thou shalt not make unto thee any graven image, or any likeness of any thing that is in the heaven above, or that is in the earth beneath, or that is in the water under the earth. (Exodus 20:4)

Kant believes it is necessary to inhibit the impetus of the imagination to prevent it advancing towards a place where the senses can see nothing, so as to strengthen the abstract feeling of a sublime and free morality. By contrast, the exhibition of spectacular images invites those who are suffering to go beyond the limits of feelings to alleviate their pain, and in so doing become docile, passive beings. It is very noticeable that in those pages where Kant writes at length on his aesthetic views, there are practically no references to images or works of art, or to literary or musical works; nor are there examples of artists, writers or musicians.

In his own life, Kant was faithful to his idea of inhibiting images, while on the other hand exhibiting ritual. In reality, daily life in Königsberg, a frontier town in Slav territory, gave him few opportunities to contemplate the magnificent spectacle of the arts. It was mostly given over to the austere, tedious life of traders and military men. Kant was fascinated by the cyclical and routine ritual of professors; during his academic career he gave 268 courses, of which 54 were on logic, 49 on metaphysics, 46 on physical geography, 28 on ethics and 24 on anthropology.[61] Moreover, he had few opportunities to appreciate works of art. He knew of many architectural works through illustrations and descriptions; he shared the taste of his time in favouring Classicism or Rococo and opposing the Gothic. But he could see only a few paintings in the private collections in Königsberg, where there were no examples of the great Italian masters (in some of his writing he confuses Raphael with Correggio). He could possibly have admired a few works by Rembrandt, Cranach and Dürer. It is highly symptomatic that Kant should describe the art of drawing as 'painting'. Above all, he enjoyed poetry, but it is probable he never read Goethe, his contemporary. Kant did not appreciate the delirium of images and figures, being more drawn to the ritual and ceremonious melancholy of abstract knowledge. He did not play a musical instrument, and preferred instrumental to orchestral music. There was only one image in his study: a portrait of Rousseau!

In spite of everything, Kant was extraordinarily sensitive to the myth of sublime melancholy, to which he felt greatly attracted. Yet he did not allow the myth to absorb him: he circled around it constantly, and made great efforts to delineate its outlines and borders. The borders separating us from the unknown are generally recognizable by the fortifications and the vigilant spirits posted in its sentry boxes and watch towers. Kant's critical work is one of those wonderful defensive walls whose construction required all the efforts of perhaps the most lucid of modern thinkers. But his sublime melancholy left lasting scars on the great philosophical structure – real scars in modern culture, which glimpses its identity in them. In order to observe this fact in Kant's imposing edifice, one of the most sophisticated monuments of modernity, I have privileged a genetic explanation, seeking a continuity in his thought while to a certain extent ignoring the differing circumstances and changes in the process of constructing his system. I have done so to illustrate the occasionally paradoxical connections between melancholy and the sublime, madness and aesthetic pleasure, oneiric visions and poetic genius. As Wolf Lepenies has pointed out, even in his treatment of the sublime, Kant demonstrates the pragmatic nature of his thought: his exaltation of melancholy or of the sublime was not an appeal for isolation or solitude, although neither was it a dissolution of the individual into society: 'To be sufficient for oneself, and consequently to have no need of society, without at the same time being unsociable, i.e. without flying from it, is something bordering the sublime.'[62] To paraphrase, we can say that his was an 'anti-melancholic melancholy', controlled but not artificial, taken to the precise limit beyond which the sublime tips over into illness. For Kant, this 'unsociable sociability' is a motivating force behind social development.[63]

AS AN OLD man, Kant read with great interest a book which popularized 'the art of prolonging human life' written by Christoph Wilhelm Hufeland, entitled *Makrobiotik*. Throughout his life, Kant was obsessed with health and his bodily functions; he desperately wished to live a long life and to postpone for as long as possible his immersion in eternity. Hufeland's book downplayed the theory of humours and nervous mechanics in favour of a stress on vitalist principles. Kant must have recognized himself in the symptoms of melancholy described in *Makrobiotik* as being typical of obstinate men with profound characters, strong emotions that do not reveal themselves and a low level of enthusiasm which means that even the strongest stimuli do not easily pierce them, although if such stimuli succeed, their impression is hard to erase or revert; they are people with an intense inner life, sad and little inclined to joy and conviviality, but lovers of silence, self-absorption and solitude. As soon as he had finished reading the book, Kant wrote to Hufeland to congratulate him and explain that he himself, since he had a sunken, narrow chest, had always been naturally predisposed towards hypochondria. Kant confessed to him that as a young man, this predisposition led him to feel a disappointment with life that he managed to overcome by considering that its causes could be entirely mechanical:

> although I felt my chest to be heavy and full, my head was clear and happy, and this happiness did not fail to show itself in society, not with fits and starts as is usual with hypochondriacal individuals, but in a natural, intentional way.[64]

Kant succeeded in controlling the threat of melancholy. His thought also managed to delimit and define it, but he never could or wished to enter its realm. The philosopher never found the language to guide him though the terrible but attractive darkness of sublime madness: that language was not within his grasp. During those same years another great German creative genius found the keys that opened the door to melancholy and made them known through one of the most astonishing pieces of music ever written: the final movement of the quartet Opus 18, No. 6, by Beethoven, composed in Vienna between 1798 and 1800. Beethoven did not usually give titles to the movements in his works, but in this case he made an exception and added a title in Italian: 'La malinconia'. Nowadays, listening to that movement allows us to enter into the dark world that Kant intuited. Most probably Kant never heard this extraordinary music, which opens with an agonizing *adagio* featuring a very brief theme that is not developed and is the expression of the painful failure of an image fixed in the mind, dialoguing with itself through diminuendos and crescendos and alternating high and low strings until it culminates in an acute cry. It is followed by an accelerated, maniacal section, which is like a frenzied dance illustrating a contrived joy. The *allegretto* Kant never heard takes us back once more to the agonized bemusement of the first theme, which it emerges from following another anguished cry as it dissolves into the tumultuous and obsessive *prestissimo* with which the music attempts in vain to conceal infinite sadness. In reality, Kant was no great music lover, although he occasionally attended a concert. He thought that music could not express ideas, only feelings.[65] To a certain extent, Kant's critical rationalism made him deaf with regard to romantic mysteries, but as his life was drawing to its close, anxiety again led him to write about feelings and mental functions. Hufeland's book was the excuse for Kant to add an appendix on the topics of sickness and hypochondria to his book *The Conflict of the Faculties* (1798). His point of departure is the exaltation 'of the power the soul has of being, by its own determination, the master of its morbid feelings'. Hypochondria, Kant here explains, is a sense of terror at the ills that can afflict humanity, without its being able to confront them; it is also a kind of frenzy brought on by an illness our feelings cannot discern, but is represented in the imagination as an evil lying in wait. In his book Kant yet again stresses the power of the rational mind over those melancholic feelings that overwhelm those who plunge into deep meditation; he recommended alternating serious thought with mechanical imaginative games. However, the best cure for hypochondria is, Kant wrote, a 'diet of one's own thoughts', since it is useless for the *Heautontimoroumenos* (the 'self-executioner') to ask any doctor for help if he does not have the courage to make the effort himself.[66] Instead of listening to his own inner melancholy, Kant offers a precise prescription:

> A reasonable thinking person does not allow such melancholy to continue to exist, but asks himself – when anxieties afflict him which threaten to deteriorate into chimeras, that is: imaginary complaints – if there are grounds for its existence. If he does not find a valid cause for his fear, or sees that there is, after all, nothing that can be done to eliminate it if such a cause should really exist, he ought to acknowledge his inner feelings and return to the order of the day.[67]

This mental diet worked well for Kant for another six years, until towards the end of 1803 when he fell gravely ill: one day he fainted, then lost his appetite and became so weak that he spent many hours in bed, sleeping on and off. 'But he was awakened', his friend Wasianski tells us, 'by terrifying dreams that could almost be called hallucinations'; and when he was awake he suffered an anxiety crisis.[68] For the first time in his long life, Kant's mind was perceiving strange feelings that brought him perilously close to

the abyss of melancholy. It is unlikely that they aroused any sublime feelings in him, because he was not now firmly bound to the
mast of the ship of life and his head was in serious danger of being
taken over by the sirens of the great beyond. However, throughout
his life Kant was in contact with that disturbing otherness that so
fascinated him, with that other Immanuel Kant who, possibly in
dark nights, spoke of what was forbidden, loved a sublime woman
and gave himself up to melancholic madness. Possibly this is why,
as Borowski informs us, he often told his friends that he had absolutely no wish to live his life again if he had to repeat his existence,
starting it in the same way from the beginning.[69] The first version
of his life had been melancholic; any repetition could plunge him
into ennui.

The Spleen of Capitalism:
Weber and the Pagan Ethic

... beneath the splenetic dome of the sky, their feet
dragging in the dust of a ground as desolate as that sky,
they walked along with the resigned features of those
condemned forever to hope.

Charles Baudelaire, 'Le Spleen de Paris', VI[1]

Far from his home and family, Max Weber turned fifty in the small Swiss town of Ascona, on the shores of Lake Maggiore. The rigorous, ascetic German sociologist, famous for his definition of the Protestant ethic as the spiritual basis of capitalism, came to this region of the Swiss Alps in 1914, possibly as an escape from the boredom of his daily life. Ascona was a beautiful, strange place that was, according to Weber's wife Marianne, a place of refuge for a most extravagant group of individuals that loathed bourgeois society: anarchists, hedonists who loved nature, vegetarians, radical psychoanalysts and artists fascinated by eroticism and free love.[2] Max Weber's presence in Ascona was no accident. He travelled there aware that he was immersing himself in a culture that contradicted both his vocation and his spirit, which had been nurtured in the conservative academic atmosphere of Heidelberg. He went to the aid of his friend Frieda Gross, who found herself in serious trouble as participant and victim of a lively erotic movement led by her husband, the psychiatrist Doctor Otto Gross, a brilliant but rebellious disciple of Freud's. If Max Weber was fleeing boredom, he certainly succeeded: he plunged into the eye of a politico-erotic hurricane riven with the most complicated family, criminal and intellectual intrigues.[3]

Max's friend had an anarchist lover who had been jailed in Zurich. Her husband, Otto Gross, had encouraged the relationship, and had also been arrested and interned in an asylum. Otto's own father, a renowned criminologist, had accused his son of being a psychopath, and had brought a court case against Frieda Gross to strip her of her rights over her children. The proof that Otto was a psychopath were his ravings about free love, his anarchism, his exaggerated praise of matriarchy and the consequent proclamation that his wife was free to have children with whomever she wished. Doctor Carl Gustav Jung had signed a certificate authorizing the Berlin police to arrest the rebel. Max Weber was tireless in helping Gross's wife defend her maternal rights as a mother. He also helped another Ascona resident, the eccentric Countess Franziska zu Reventlow – a rebel aristocrat renowned for her sexual liberty – in complicated divorce proceedings.

It might seem astonishing that the dry, sober sociology professor should become involved with this world. Max Weber's link to these counter-cultural circles originates from his friendship with the famous von Richthofen sisters, Else and Frieda. The former had been a student of his at university and was the wife of Edgar Jaffé, one of Weber's closest collaborators. Frieda was married to an English philologist, Ernest Weekley, and had once had an intense loving relationship with Otto Gross, and later became the wife of D. H. Lawrence, the notorious author of *Lady Chatterley's Lover*. Else had also been Doctor Gross's lover, something of which Weber had disapproved and which had made him jealous, since he was secretly in love with his former disciple. Max Weber's involvement with this intensely eroticized environment was regarded by his wife as an experience that allowed the sociologist 'an enriching insight into the strange world of people with attitudes entirely different from his own.'[4] This social atmosphere brought Weber into direct contact with hedonism and madness, two aspects of life which also affected him personally in a profound and long-lasting way. However, as we shall see, far from enriching his vision, the dramatic confrontation brought about a singular blindness that prevented him from recognizing that eroticism and melancholy, those strange forms of the pagan ethic, also formed part of the spirit of capitalism.

Max Weber had acquired a solid, puritanical ideal of sexual morality. In some fascinating pages of her husband's biography, Marianne Weber describes the ethic that, in the sociologist's view, ought to govern sexual unions and marriage. This is a Protestant ethic that could be seen as equivalent in the erotic field to the puritan morality Weber had described as a fundamental element of the capitalist spirit. In Heidelberg at the dawn of the twentieth century, Marianne tells us, there was a determined assault on traditional values that imposed respect for the law, duty and asceticism in sexual relations. Many young people were searching for a 'new ethic' that would allow the liberalization of sexual morality to avoid the stifling of natural instincts and the repression of vital currents flowing through the body. Max Weber listened carefully to these new arguments about free love, but firmly defended established morality, marriage as an absolute ideal based on love and on the sacrifice to an ethic of erotic union. Any person unwilling to accept the ethical ideal – Weber believed – is at fault with regard to the superior order that presides over all social morality. Consequently, sensual pleasure ought not to be an end in itself, not even as aesthetically sublimated eroticism. Anybody avoiding their 'duty' could become frivolous or brutal. The Kantian origin of these ideas is obvious; Weber himself correctly affirmed that Kant had come very close to the Protestant asceticism and puritan ethic typical of the capitalist spirit.[5] Max Weber followed a similar path, and is described by his wife as a virtuous gentleman who defended the sexual ethic against the 'forces of dissolution' driven by socialist theories of marriage, Sigmund Freud's psychiatry, Nietzsche's philosophy and other feminist and pedagogical theories. Marianne Weber dismisses the new theories, which in her view are easy to refute, although she admits 'their hearts were touched' because their friends adopted them.

In 1907 the new ethic promoted by Doctor Otto Gross was accepted by Else, Max Weber's disciple and wife of his close col-laborator, Edgar Jaffé. She had also become Gross's lover and was expecting his child. To further try Weber's patience, the review he edited with Jaffé, the *Archiv für Sozialwissenschaften und Sozialpolitik*, was sent an essay by Gross in which he expounded his theories at length and criticized Freud's theses on the need for repression, inhibition and sublimation. Weber refused outright to publish the essay, and wrote a horrified letter explaining his reasons. The letter, addressed to Jaffé but sent to his wife Else (who in all probability suggested to her lover that he submit the essay in the first place) offers interesting evidence of Weber's puritanism. The letter confesses at the outset that it will seem to support the position of somebody defending a conventional ethic, that of an 'ethical Pharisee'. It goes on to criticize Freud and refers to a 'nause-ating concoction of "holy God" with various unappetizing erotica'. Whilst accepting that one day the present poverty of Freud's thought might have something to contribute, Weber indignantly denies that psychoanalytic ideas have ethical consequences that challenge the established norms by proving that to observe these norms implies an unhealthy repression. He mocks the 'nervous ethic' of Gross, who seeks, according to Weber, 'that I give free rein to every stirring of my desires and of my instinctual life, no matter how low-down it may be . . . because otherwise my precious nerves might be injured'. Weber considers that every ethic, from primitive Christianity to that of Kant, starts from such a pessimistic judge-ment of human nature that no Freudian revelation about the unconscious could add anything worse or more terrible. Weber does not think he is learning anything new, and therefore does not believe that the psychoanalytic form of confession can help him in the field of ethics by reminding him of some aberrant sexual behaviour a servant might have had towards him as a child. In other words, Weber accepts the heavy burden of a terrible original sin whose echoes are to be found in the 'dirty impulses' that are 'repressed' or 'forgotten'. The 'new ethic', on the other hand, refuses to accept the immoral nature of these primordial impulses.[6]

We can even find traces of this sense of guilt in the letter proposing marriage that Max writes to Marianne early in 1893. In it he confesses that he tries 'with difficulty and varying success, to tame the elemental passions with which nature has endowed me'. The letter is an ascetic call to a 'high-minded comrade' to renounce all passion, not to be taken in by 'unclear and mystical moods' and to control her feelings in order to behave with 'sobriety'.[7] This sobriety was taken to such lengths that Weber and his wife apparently never consummated their marriage. It therefore comes as no surprise that the fear of uncontrollable nocturnal emissions should contribute to Weber's insomnia.[8] What seems to me interesting is that Weber did not consider the puritan ethic simply as a historical problem that he grappled with as a sociologist – sixteenth-century Calvinism as the basis of the capitalist spirit – but also as a topic that was alive in his own day, and indeed in his own life. For the German sociologist, the pagan ethic was not only a topic connected to the ancient orgiastic expressions of religious exoticism or to the sexual aspects of the other-worldly irrational mysticism of some oriental sects: in Europe, Romanticism, socialism and anarchism contributed to the renaissance of the pagan morality that so disturbed Weber.

His concern is understandable: Weber thought that the Protestant ethic – especially Calvinist puritan asceticism – was the backbone of the modern spirit. Inner-worldly rationalism had given Western man an ascetic vocation which allowed him the efficient regulation of the capitalist way of life. He had demonstrated that this modern spirit only progressed at the expense of magic and the retreat of the other-worldly religious traditions linked to mysticism, stoic escapism and hedonism. Symptomatically, Weber employs a metaphor from Baudelaire, the 'holy prostitution of the soul', when he equates the mystical flight from the world to the loving surrender without an object, not for mankind but for the surrender itself.[9] The new pagan ethic that spread throughout Europe at the end of the nineteenth century was only other-worldly up to a point: it would be more exact to call it *counter-worldly*. Weber had already pointed out the non-modern nature of the Catholic Counter-Reformation: 'Capitalism cannot make use of the labour of those who practise the doctrine of undisciplined *liberum arbitrium*.'[10] How could capitalism now face up to the challenge of this counter-worldly culture? This contradiction, which Weber experienced personally, has been cited as one of the tensions that appear to negate the progressive rationalizing disenchantment meant to permeate modern society: the appearance of the so-called counter-cultural currents of the mid-twentieth century has led sociologists such as Daniel Bell to think that modern society suffers from irreconcilable incompatibilities.[11] However, these contradictions are nothing new: they are rooted in what I have called the counter-worldly culture that Max Weber confronted, which was fed by nineteenth-century romantic traditions. If Weber were alive today, at the start of the twenty-first century, he would see that the Protestant ethic has been packed away and replaced by hedonism. As Daniel Bell wrote: 'The cultural, if not moral, justification of capitalism has become hedonism, the idea of pleasure as a way of life.'[12] How then is capitalism to function without its puritan ethic?

THE HEDONISTIC AND anarchist spirit held a great fascination for Max Weber. His trip to Ascona in 1914 is very significant in this respect (he had already visited the small town the previous year). In addition to his need for rest and a desire to help his friends,

Weber was very curious about the counter-worldly culture that had taken up residence in Ascona and made it a place of pilgrimage.[13] Could Weber have reflected on the possible positive functions of the fight against inner-worldly culture – ascetic, patriarchal, puritan, disciplined – typical of the bourgeois spirit? During that cold 1914 spring, Weber sat by the fireside for many hours to converse with Otto Gross's wife: 'She has a great need to talk things out,' Weber writes. 'Last week she visited her lover in jail. He, too, has a religious faith in an unjealous future of truly "free" – inwardly liberated – love.' Weber in return defended a 'gentlemanly' attitude with regard to jealous emotions, and rejected her 'insane waste of emotional energy.'[14] In his first book, *The Secondary Functions of the Brain* (1902), Otto Gross had developed an important theory about the existence of two opposing mental types.[15] The first of these corresponds to individuals with a vast but superficial understanding that is quick to grasp facts and put them to use in the short term, but suffers from a primitive, trivial emotional life lacking the richness of an erotic imagination linked to the higher aesthetic and ethical powers. The second type, characterized by a profound emotional life, is slow to understand and apply facts, being more focussed on symbolic abstraction and the harmony of experience, and distancing itself from effective social action in favour of aesthetics and visionary and idealistic attitudes. According to Gross, these two types illustrate the opposition between the businessman and the man of ideas, the man of civilization and the man of culture, the person who is a realistic fighter and the solitary creator of images. The first is characteristic of the stormy times during which empires are established; the second is a product of the high culture developed as a result of empire. This duality became a commonplace of a wide variety of intellectual expressions of the time, both in its psychological form and in its social and cultural variants. We can assume that Gross saw Weber as a representative of the first mental category, whilst considering himself an example of the second.

Freud admired Otto Gross as one of his most brilliant follow-ers, although in 1909 he came to the conclusion that his disciple's ideas had become a threat to the psychoanalytical movement. The previous year, on Freud's recommendation, Gross had been interned in the Burghölzli clinic in Switzerland – where he had previously spent some time – for a detox cure for his addiction to morphine. During his stay he was analysed by Carl Gustav Jung. By this time, Gross had already developed his most radical ideas, ones that took him close to anarchism, the exaltation of sexual freedom and therapeutic practices that (as rumour had it) were orgiastic in nature. There was no lack of scandals surround-ing the conflictive personality of Doctor Gross. In 1906 in Ascona, a patient of his who suffered from depression committed suicide by poisoning herself with a drug he had supplied; this incident aroused the suspicions of the local police, who imagined some strange anarchist plot. In 1911 another very similar event took place, when his lover Sophie Benz, who was mentally unstable, also killed herself. The therapeutic sessions that Gross organized in an empty barn were truly experimental rituals that sought dis-inhibition and liberation, but aroused all kinds of suspicion. Since 1902 there had also been in Ascona another strange therapeutic centre, the sanatorium of Monte Verità, where natural cures were promoted with mud, water or sun bathing, a vegetarian diet or fasting, all inspired by a mixture of mystical theories, theosophy and Wagnerism. All sorts of people came to Ascona either for cures, to convalesce or simply rest: among them for example were the so-called *Naturmenschen* – like the famous Gusto Gräser – who wandered around half-naked and lived in caves or ruins; Hermann Hesse, who took mud baths in the naturist sanatorium to cure his alcoholism; the celebrated anarchist Pyotr Kropotkin, who visited Ascona every summer between 1908 and 1913, sup-posedly to receive treatment from his friend, the Jewish doctor Raphael Friedeberg; and Rudolf Laban, the great maestro of modern dance, who in Monte Verità in 1913 founded the Schule für Lebenskunst.[16]

To Weber it was obvious that these anti-worldly movements were a threat to the process of disenchantment driven by the progress of calculation, forecasting and secular reasoning. In his famous lecture on 'Science as a Vocation' (1919) he mocked those modern intellectuals whom he saw as charlatans or gullible, who, faced with the retreat of religion, seek to substitute it by constructing

> a sort of domestic chapel with small sacred images from all over the world, or they produce surrogates through all sorts of psychic experiences to which they ascribe the dignity of mystic holiness, which they peddle in the book market.

He did, however, recognize that certain adolescent communities function without subterfuge, as 'a religious, cosmic, or mystical relation', although he doubted whether these new forms of community added any dignity to purely human communal relationships. He ended his lecture by stressing that nothing is gained by 'yearning and tarrying': one has to get down to work. 'This, however, is plain and simple, if each finds and obeys the demon who holds the fibers of his very life.'[17]

Weber did not always meet his demon. Occasionally he seemed instead to want to run away from him, and when he did meet him, he did not know how to compromise: in 1898, at the age of only 34, his demon let him lapse into an acute mental illness, which forced him to abandon his academic work for many years, and from which he never entirely recovered. His wife described his nervous breakdown as a 'descent to hell'.[18] The demon that made Weber an ascetic hero, and a model of sexual abstinence and devotion to his academic career, often left him prey to melancholy. For example, Edward Baumgarten recalls a conversation between Weber and his wife that took place towards the end of the sociologist's life:

Max: Tell me, can you think of yourself as a mystic?
Marianne: That would certainly be the *last* thing I could think of. Can you conceive of it for yourself?
Max: It could even be that I *am* one. Just as I have 'dreamt' more in my life than one really ought to be allowed, I am also not really *quite* securely at home anywhere. It is as though I could (and wanted) to pull myself back from everything, and completely.[19]

Weber was able to accept this in private. But in his public life he presented the image with which his friend Karl Jaspers sought to immortalize him after his death, when he described him as 'the new kind of man': 'He was the modern human being who permitted no concealment, who finds in this veracity life's impetus, allowing no escape into despair.'[20] The reality was different: Weber had abandoned his ascetic demon not only during his intimate mystical outbursts, but also when he allowed himself to fall into the arms of eroticism.

When Max Weber arrived in Ascona in 1914 he had already begun a romantic relationship with the Swiss pianist Mina Tobler the previous year. And in 1910, in Venice, he had declared his love for Else Jaffé. Although she rejected him on that occasion, they did begin a relationship several years later. Weber was simply a typical man of the Victorian era, whose hypocrisy was the 'homage vice offers to virtue' according to La Rochefoucauld's fortunate expression. Or, as Peter Gay has it in his Freudian version, the 'tribute that the ego paid to the superego.'[21] Of course I have no wish to condemn Weber's hypocrisy, merely to stress the fact that the sociologist did not succeed in critically integrating a relatively common form of survival into his vision of the ascetic puritan ethic as the cultural basis of capitalism. In contrast, as Peter Gay points out, Freud realized that a certain amount of 'cultural hypocrisy' was indispensable to sustain civilization.[22] Weber did not like

Freud, but even in Kant's transcendental puritan ethic, which he inherited, he could have found a reflection on the topic, which also reflects one of the forms of the capitalist spirit. The sociologist who so highly praised the inner-worldly ethic could have read in the final pages of the *Anthropology* (1798) a charming and instructive other-worldly, or more exactly extra-terrestrial, story. Kant imagines that on another planet there are rational beings who can only think out loud, both when they are awake and asleep, and equally when they are on their own or in company. Kant speculates on the kind of behaviour these beings might have, when they are incapable of having thoughts that they could keep to themselves. If they were not all 'as pure as angels' it is impossible to believe that they could live together, agree and respect one another. This leads to the logical conclusion about human beings in this world: it is part of their original composition 'to explore the thoughts of others but to withhold one's own; a neat quality that does not fail to progress gradually from *dissimulation* to *intentional deception* and finally to *lying*'. Kant, rejecting the misanthropy that this story suggests, concludes by affirming that contempt for this situation betrays the innate existence in mankind of a rational moral basis that drives them to fight against this propensity to falsehood.[23]

To a certain extent, Weber wanted to be a Kantian extraterrestrial condemned to speak the truth and to behave like a puritan ascetic. But he lived on this planet and was contaminated by the mundanity of his century. Doubtless he was aware of the paradox implicit in the secularizing influence of the wealth that the same puritan ethic helped accumulate. In order to illustrate this paradox, Weber turns to the Methodists: John Wesley had pointed out that religion necessarily produces both industry and frugality, which in turn generate wealth. But as wealth increased – Wesley believed – there was also an increase in pride, anger, carnal desires and in general all forms of worldly love.[24] Weber had succumbed to worldly love, as is reflected even in the letters he sent his wife during his trip to Ascona and other places in Switzerland. He writes of a 'world full of enchantresses, charms, trickery, and desire for happiness' and of an excursion to the island of Ufenau (in the lake of Zurich) with 'this girl who is different but seems so "noble" in her reserved and delicately rapturous way' (he is referring to Mina Tobler). He spends his time reading essays and novels; he reads in French *Marie Donadieu*, a novel by Charles-Louis Philippe, which appears to him a 'critique of eroticism on a very high level', even if it is an inadequate 'expression of the wealth and the greatness of an extra-erotic life'. In general, his letters show a certain Tolstoyan asceticism which quite possibly conceals an attraction for pagan hedonism. With his friend Frieda Gross he spends hours discussing many different topics: eroticism, politics, ethics. On one occasion, Weber writes in a letter to his wife, he had a lengthy discussion with Frieda about 'lies'. His friend cannot understand why Weber believes one should not 'simply lie on the witness stand to "enemies"'; she thinks only friends have the right to the truth. Weber argues that he could not be sure that someone who had such an idea could really be the 'friend' he or she claimed to be. Frieda then asks if that is the reason why he seems so distant. Weber confesses that the reason stems from his own experience: 'I could under certain circumstances be quite fond of specifically "erotic" women, as she herself must have noticed, but I would never form any inner attachment to one or count on her friendship'. Weber points out that only an 'erotic' man is valued by this kind of woman, and that he would never trust their comradeship. This obviously displeased Mrs Gross, and so they left the discussion there.[25]

Weber does not reveal the truth to his wife Marianne, although he hints that he has been transported to a 'strange, fabulous world'. At the foot of the magnificent Alps he allows himself to be enchanted by the magical beauty of colours filtered by the cloudy climate, with a sublime mountain background and its grey twilight tones. When he turns fifty, Weber writes to Marianne: 'My God!

I am starting my fiftieth year! I still cannot believe it, because I am still so strangely youthful!'[26] Yet he was to live only another six years, during which time he was to taste the honey of worldly sensuality but also the bitter experiences of the Great War, which broke out only a few months later. In Ascona, Max Weber was a nineteenth-century man contemplating, fascinated but uncomprehending, the arrival of a new century filled with a mixture of violence and hedonism.

ACCORDING TO MAX Weber, the capitalist spirit was spurred on by a puritan ethic that favoured the elimination of all those magical practices aimed at obtaining God's grace. The result was the profound isolation of the individual, whose interior life implied a rejection of all of culture's sensual and emotional elements. Weber explains that this is one of the roots of the pessimistic, disenchanted individualism typical of the national character of peoples with a puritan past.[27] The example he provides is very revealing: John Bunyan's *The Pilgrim's Progress*, the most widely read book in puritan literature. The spiritual isolation suffered by Christian, the pilgrim who escapes from the City of Destruction, leads him to sever his links with the world and daily life. There is a passage in his pilgrimage that seems to me particularly striking, as it employs the metaphor of the iron cage. Christian is led by his guide the Interpreter to a very dark room where 'a man in an iron cage' is seated.[28] It is impossible not to recall that at the end of *The Protestant Ethic and the Spirit of Capitalism* Weber quotes Richard Baxter to the effect that to puritans, concern for external goods ought to be as light as a slender cloak on the shoulders of the saint, which can be easily cast aside. However, Weber comments, fate meant that the cloak instead became an iron cage.[29] In fact, the expression is a paraphrase Talcott Parsons permitted himself in his translation of Weber's *The Protestant Ethic*. Weber does not speak of an iron cage, but of a box or dwelling place as tough as steel ('*ein stahlhartes Gehäuse*'), and is referring to the solitary enclosure of man surrounded by a mass and massive petrification of possessions and goods.

For Bunyan, the iron cage is a metaphor for melancholy. When Pilgrim asks the man shut in the cage the reasons for his misfortune, the man replies:

> I was once a fair and flourishing professor, both in mine own eyes, and also in the eyes of others . . . I am now a man of despair, and I am shut up in it, as in this iron cage. I cannot get out. Oh, now I cannot!

The man once met all the demands of his profession and believed he was destined for the Celestial City; but he abandoned sobriety, tempted the Devil, sinned against the light of the world and God's kindness, and let his heart grow so hard that now it is too late for him to repent. The man in the cage explains the causes of his fall:

> For the lusts, pleasures, and profits of this world; in the enjoyment of which I did then promise myself much delight; but now every one of those things also bite me, and gnaw me like a burning worm.

It is difficult to understand how the puritan and Calvinist call to sever all worldly, sensual ties could connect to the most advanced forms of social organization. Max Weber recognizes that this is a strange mystery, but maintains it can be explained by the dogmatic insistence that the world exists only to glorify the Lord, and by the Calvinist denial of any conflict between individual and existential ethics.[30] This topic has led to many doubts and arguments, but I do not wish to discuss it directly here. I prefer instead to make a detour and comment on the fact that Max Weber distanced himself from the theme of melancholy, something which he hinted at when he recognized that the puritan doctrine caused suffering and anxiety because it exacerbated the inner solitude of individuals.[31]

However, the relation between puritanism and melancholy was something that had been widely debated since the seventeenth century. First, there are the anti-puritan critics who point out the terrible way in which religious excesses condemn believers to falling into melancholic madness. Second, there exist the recommendations of the puritans themselves as to how to overcome the melancholic anxieties brought about by the recognition of the inevitable repercussions of original sin and mankind's submission to the impenetrable mystery of predestination. From the seventeenth century on, it became a commonplace in England to associate melancholy with the religious enthusiasm of the puritan and Pietist sects. It was supposed that excessive zeal in the pursuance of faith brought on one of the most extensive illnesses, spleen, which was in fact so common it was known as the 'English disease'.[32] In his 1717 essay on the treatment of religious melancholy, Robert Blakeway recommended avoiding excessive religious fervour, explaining that 'it is absolutely false that the Christian Religion interdicts the Gratification of any of our Faculties in earthly Pleasures and Enjoyements.'[33]

Even puritan theologians recognized the dangers of excessive religious humiliations, sadnesses and duties. Richard Baxter himself recommended that the divine truth revealed to pilgrims should be spread 'not . . . rashly, nor with self flattery, nor with melancholy terrors', as he says in the same book that Weber cites to refer to the light weight of the cloak of external goods, a cloak that is transformed into tough, modern steel armour.[34] Of course, Baxter did not believe that evangelical piety was the cause of the black humours, but he was concerned at the harmful effects on people already predisposed to them:

I have often known weak-headed people (that be not able to order their thoughts), and many melancholy people, guilty of the other; that is, of thinking too much, and too seriously and intensely on good and holy things, whereby they have overthrown their reason, and been distracted. And here I would give all such weak-headed, melancholy persons this warning, that whereas in my Book of Rest, I so much press a constant course of heavenly meditation, I do intend it only for sound heads, and not for the melancholy, that have weak heads, and are unable to bear it. That may be their sin, which to others is a very great duty; while they think to do that which they cannot do, they will but disable themselves for that which they can do. I would therefore advise those melancholy persons whose minds are so troubled, and heads weakened, that they are in danger of overthrowing their understandings (which usually begins in multitudes of scruples, and restlessness of mind, and continual fears, and blasphemous temptations; where it begins with these, distraction is at hand, if not prevented), that they forbear meditation, as being no duty to them, though it be to others.[35]

The theme of melancholy demonstrates one great difficulty in Weber's interpretation: how is it possible for the capitalist spirit to grow out of religious attitudes that condemn sensual pleasures and the enjoyment of earthly goods, and which brought the puritans to the edge of an abyss of anxiety, melancholy and madness? Supposedly, faced with the crisis created by the tremendous uncertainty of salvation after death, puritanism unintentionally offered as an alternative the earthly pursuit of a vocation, in the shape of ascetic tasks aimed at the accumulation of wealth. This explanation is hardly convincing, and has been criticized on well-founded grounds.[36] It is not enough to interpret melancholy as a way of pushing the troubled faithful to undertake earthly labours in a rational manner. Melancholy is a kind of catastrophic flood sweeping over the earth, a consequence of a rigid religious practice that denies all certainty of the posthumous salvation of souls and obliges the faithful to live beneath the ominous shadow of original sin. Without having any prior intention of creating an existential crisis, in its pastoral advice the Protestant ethic offered a lifeline to the desperate, drowning victim, as MacKinnon has pointed out.[37] This same author maintains that in reality the Protestant ethic as epitomized by the *Westminster Confession* (1648) did not take on board Calvinist ideas about predestination, and so avoided the supposed crisis arising from the lack of proof about the post-mortem future of souls. Since he did not properly understand this, Weber mistakenly came to believe that Calvinism had special characteristics that made it the spiritual engine of capitalism.[38]

In addition, Weber failed to explain a cultural dimension – melancholy – that was one of the foundational ideas of capitalist modernity.[39] If Weber had more closely analysed the metaphor of the iron cage in *The Pilgrim's Progress*, he would have discovered the melancholy roots of puritan faith. But he would also have understood that melancholic anxiety was a widespread cultural malaise that contained nothing that would drive people more towards the Protestant ethic than towards any other means of escape, religious or otherwise, from the iron cage, such as for example the Catholic Counter-Reformation or mysticism. The Protestant ethos did not have a monopoly on melancholy. In fact, melancholy was part of an ancient pagan ethos that the Baroque and reformist renaissance cultures were steeped in. This melancholy ethos was still alive in Max Weber's day, as it had been adopted and recreated both by the Enlightenment philosophers and the Romantics. It was the ethos of the sublime that Kant and Schiller had exalted, and with which Weber had a contradictory relationship of affinity and rejection. The ethos of the sublime contained that mix of aestheticism, sensuality and melancholy that so greatly alarmed Weber, and whose relationship with the capitalist spirit he could never understand.

MAX WEBER HAD a profound respect for the moral order on which the family and social relationships of his time were based. He was always a conservative gentleman ready to defend the rules and laws of honour in intense verbal duels; as a young man he had even fought real duels with weapons and had proudly shown off a scar on the cheek left by a fight.[40] On the other hand, in his research he habitually denied the existence of historical or social laws, and was more interested in the infinite number of links and interactions between the different spheres of cultural and social life. It is symptomatic that to refer to the relationships between different aspects of this he should choose to employ the famous literary metaphor made popular by one of Goethe's novels: the titular 'elective affinities' (*Wahlverwandtschaften*). For example, to reassure those who feared that modernity would bring with it an excess of individualistic democracy and erode aristocratic and authoritarian values, he insisted it was ridiculous to suppose that advanced capitalism – as it exists in the United States and is coming to Russia – had any elective affinity with democracy or liberty.[41] In *The Protestant Ethic* elective affinities occupy a fundamental methodological place: Weber maintains that, faced with the tremendous confusion of mutual influences between the material basis, socio-political organization and the spiritual manifestations of the Reformation, the only way to proceed is to investigate whether any elective affinities can be established between certain religious expressions and the professional ethic. Weber concludes that this can help clarify the way in which, as a consequence of these elective affinities, the religious movement influenced the development of materialist culture. In fact, the entire second half of the book consists of the detailing of the elective affinities between the professional ethic of ascetic Protestantism and the development of capitalism. Weber uses the idea of elective affinities to skirt round the thesis which holds that capitalism is a result of the Reformation, and the affirmation that the capitalist spirit could only arise thanks to it. In his translation of *The Protestant Ethic*, Talcott Parsons replaced the use of 'elective affinities' as a metaphor with the simpler term 'correlations'.[42] He did this to try to remove the strange presence of a romantic myth in Weber's work, but as a result he deprived it of much of its charm and magic.

The use of a metaphor such as 'elective affinities' is very revealing: it refers to a mysterious amorous attraction that undermines the ethical foundation of modern marriage. In Goethe's *Elective Affinities* the boring matrimonial order rigidly encased in the daily life of the wealthy landowners is destroyed by the sudden irruption of profound erotic affinities between the married couple and two characters who arrive on their estate: Ottilie, the beautiful but melancholy young woman, and the Captain, who has a scientific bent and a great organizing ability. But the husband, Eduard, allows his love to drag him tumultuously to a tragic end. In the novel, matrimony is like an edifice: to consolidate it, lime is needed, since, as the mason, one of the secondary characters, says in the book: 'as men who are naturally inclined to one another hold together better when they are cemented by the law, so too bricks . . .'.[43] The main protagonists discuss the dissolving powers of a chemical force, elective affinity, that can even destroy hard limestone. Subsequently they themselves feel the force of forbidden affinities: some choose to reject the strength of passion; others decide – to their own and others' misfortune – to fling themselves into an erotic extramarital relationship.

I wonder if when he spoke of elective affinities, Weber was possibly thinking of the powerful attraction that both spleen and hedonism exerted over the newly emerging actors in modern capitalism, alongside exacerbated capitalism and the uncontrolled democratic freedoms that undermined respect for traditional moral values. He himself established elective affinities with both his young disciple Else and with the melancholy that ate away at him inside. It is impossible that in using the allegory of elective affinities Weber did not also have the image of his own intellectual and personal conflicts. The similarity between his situation and that outlined in Goethe's book is too obvious for the sociologist not to have reflected on it. The tedious academic life in Heidelberg was similar to the existence of Goethe's characters, stuck in the boring prosperity typical of great landowners, embourgeoisified Junkers who spend their time taking delightful walks in the woods and gardens surrounding their mansion, and in planning new paths and pavilions, steeped in a decadent mix of aesthetic attitudes and utilitarian projects. Within this Romantic context, Goethe introduces the problem of freedom: the choice (election) of certain affinities brings about the dramatic dissolution of family order, but on the other hand the decision to respect matrimonial guidelines at all costs condemns society to a dangerous ascetic boredom. The first election leads to the melancholy deaths of the lovers; the second leads to another kind of melancholy: the ennui of those who submit to the domestic bliss that comes from duty and morality. But is there such a thing as free election? It is not easy to interpret Goethe's complex novel, and it is not clear whether abandoning oneself to the forbidden affinities is a free act, or rather submission to a monstrous law of an implacably chemical nature.

Max Weber did not see that the elective affinities of modern life inevitably involved depression and ennui. Yet again we can observe that there is a blind spot in Weber's sociological eye. Was it this blindness that prevented him from reading – or if in fact he did read it, from taking into account – an extraordinary book devoted to offering a sociological interpretation of melancholy? I mean *Le Suicide*, by Émile Durkheim, published in 1897. In this book, the great French sociologist proposes a link between Protestantism and high suicide rates, and takes this as his starting point for a study of the origins and social causes of something apparently enclosed within the boundaries of individual tragedy. Beyond this link between Protestantism and suicide, Durkheim discovers a profound melancholy brought on by the exaggerated individualism and extreme weakening of the social cohesion that was based on traditional beliefs.[44] To a certain extent, Durkheim analysed the same problem which centuries earlier had so troubled puritan theologians: the disturbing affinities between the rigours of individual religious responsibility and the excesses of melancholy madness.[45] Reading Durkheim allows us to penetrate into what Weber did not want or would not see. *Le Suicide* was also a dry, harsh sociological response to a fundamental tension in nineteenth-century culture, whose different challenges and facets are to be found in Baudelaire's spleen, Freud's melancholy, Verlaine's saturnism, Kräpelin's depression, Mahler's anguish, Trakl's despair or Munch's angst, and which has its roots in the Romantic tradition.

Durkheim was interested in defining a kind of suicide that had no morbid natural cause, and was free of hereditary, racial or geographical factors. He wished to discover the moral nature of suicide – that is to say, its essentially social dimension. He was interested in precise social causes, and would not have liked to think in terms of subtle elective affinities. In order to do so, he first studied individual psychopathic states leading to suicide, which allowed him to define four types: the maniacal, melancholic, obsessive and impulsive. He observes that, in these types of madness, suicide occurs without any purely imaginary motive, the product of hallucinations, ravings or obsessions.[46] There is therefore no possibility of discovering in them any collective, social or moral tendencies. However, when Durkheim analyses egotistical suicide – the first in which he recognizes social causes – it is plain that he discovers a close link with melancholic suicide. Although he defines egotistical suicide in terms of its moral causes, he considers that the excessive affirmation of the individual ego to the detriment of the social being produces a state of melancholy. Durkheim finds that within Protestantism there is an exaggerated individualism which leads to suicidal tendencies and whose source is the disintegration of social relations. Unlike Weber, he recognizes that civilization and modernity are linked to forms of collective melancholy that contribute to a rise in suicide rates.[47] This does not occur because the anguished individual is confronting nothingness, the fact that he or she is destined to die: rather, it is a social process, a truly 'collective humour' – streams of depression, melancholy and disenchantment that do not come from any one individual, but from the state of disintegration in which society finds itself.[48] The root of this evil is not to be found in religion or in existential or metaphysical anguish, but in the 'physiological misery of the social body' which is reflected even in certain 'theoreticians of sadness' who recommend suicide, or at least encourage it by preaching disillusion and despair.[49] While he does not identify these 'theoreticians of sadness', I would venture that he had in mind Schopenhauer and Nietzsche, the Romantics and Baudelaire.

Melancholy also tinges the expressions of the second type of suicide addressed by Durkheim: the altruistic. This kind of self-sacrifice is the result of insufficient individuation, yet sadness connects it to egotistical suicide:

> Whereas the egotist is sad because he cannot see anything real in the world beyond the individual, the sadness of the intemperate altruist arises on the contrary because the individual seems to him stripped of any reality.[50]

The first type of melancholy is an incurable feeling of weariness and sad depression; the second, by contrast, is one of hope, since it considers that more beautiful vistas will open beyond this boring life. The third kind of suicide is in fact akin to the first: it is the anomic suicide of those individuals whose actions are thrown into chaos. Whereas in egotistical suicide there is a degree of absence of collective activity which appears to rob life of meaning, the anomic individual can find no social restraint for his passions and suffers because his actions lack organization. Durkheim portrays a kind of sociological theory of humours that assimilates these kinds of suicide to three 'currents' circulating through the social body: egotism ('languid melancholy'), altruism ('active renunciation') and anomie ('exasperated weariness').[51] These are not metaphors, but 'collective forces' that drive people to take their own lives: truly moral forces that mutually intertwine and assuage one another. If a balance can be struck between them, suicidal tendencies can be lessened; but what Durkheim terms 'hypercivilization' increases egotistical and anomic tendencies and 'tunes up nervous systems', rendering them excessively delicate and consequently resistant to discipline, but prey to violent irritation or exaggerated depression. In contrast to supercivilized refinements, a primitive, rude and rough culture implies excessive altruism and a lack of sensibility that facilitates the renouncing of life.[52]

It could be said, and this is something that strangely has not been recognized, that *Le Suicide* is a book about collective modern melancholy. But Durkheim exaggerates the social dimensions to such an extent that he plays down the distinctions, and his analysis lacks the subtlety needed to perceive the cultural elements. He tends to reduce the ethical to its social dimension, and sees melancholy (and suicide) as above all an effect of the lack of cohesion, disorder and disintegration of society. However, his curious theory of the balance between the different collective humours allowed him to understand that human beings could not live if they were completely averse to sadness: 'Certainly there are sorrows,' he said, 'to which we can only adapt if we love them, and the pleasure we find in them has something melancholy about it. Melancholy is only morbid when it takes up too much room in life; but a life that excludes it is equally morbid.'[53]

And so in the end Durkheim was able to accept that, between natural pathogenic phenomena and social morbidity, there existed a space filled by sadness, melancholy and longed-for death, possibly as a ransom to be paid to modern civilization. Or more exactly – Weber might have thought if he had considered the problem – as a space where the elective affinities are formed between the capitalist spirit and the hymns of the dark night that a few people such as the writer Novalis were able to hear even in the clamour of the Enlightenment.

In Goethe's novel, the elective affinities lead the sweet Ottilie to a slow-motion suicide brought on by a kind of erotic anorexia. Her self-destruction is undoubtedly a romantic way of escaping from the profound ennui invading civilization, and a sign of the malaise that goes hand-in-hand with the capitalist spirit. Level-headed Charlotte, who is no great believer in elective affinities, sees things in a realistic way that Durkheim would have applauded:

> As life draws us along . . . we think we are acting of our own volition, ourselves choosing what we shall do and what we shall enjoy; but when we look more closely we see they are only the intentions and inclinations of the age which we are being compelled to comply with.[54]

Weber did not share this harsh view but was surely right to invoke the sociological validity of elective affinities, since he was well aware it was necessary to leave an important place for liberty at the heart of social tendencies that appeared to stifle it. However, he did not understand that melancholy, as in Munch's famous 1893 engraving, is also a shout of freedom.

AS HE EXPLAINED in a letter to his fiancée in 1887, Weber thought that the exaggerated adoration of Goethe spoilt people's appreciation of other great authors such as Schiller. In particular, he thought Goethe had been unable to perceive vileness if it appeared 'in the guise of certain beautiful feelings' and in fact uses *Elective Affinities* as an example of this. Goethe, Weber believed, only understood evil if it appeared at the same time as ugliness.[55] The beauty of forbidden love hid what for the sociologist was vileness. Many years later, shortly before his death, Weber was still concerned about the disassociation between ethic and aesthetic values. In his notable lecture on 'Science as a Vocation' of 1919, he returned to the problem:

> we also know that something can be beautiful even though
> – but also *because* – it is not good. We have known this
> since Nietzsche, and you will find it earlier presented in the
> *Fleurs du mal* – as Baudelaire called his volume of poems.[56]

He also stressed the fact that something can be sacred not only even if it is not beautiful, but *because* it is not, and *to the extent* that it is not. In Weber's view, it is completely impossible scientifically to identify one value system as being truer than another from its aesthetic, religious or ethical manifestations: 'something can be true even if it is not beautiful, or sacred, or good.' Inspired by an idea of John Stuart Mill, Weber affirms resolutely that, outside of an empirical account, there is no possible resolution of the battle between the gods of different value systems. Are the ideals emanating from Baudelaire's flowers better than the values of Kant's science? Is French culture more valuable than German? Is the ethical puritan life more correct than the pagan hedonism of the Ascona anarchists? Every individual has to decide *for him or her* self who is God, and who is the Devil.[57] The various positivist theologies claim that the world has a meaning, but sooner or later they are forced to accept Saint Augustine's maxim: 'I believe it, because it is absurd' (*credo non quod, sed quia absurdum est*). To Weber, this is a 'sacrifice of the intellect' that the truly religious person reaches.[58] That is why, as Diggins has said, Weber can be considered as the Herman Melville of social science, as the first sociologist to understand that the universe has no true meaning.[59]

I should like to see Weber's extreme relativism as a way of affirming mankind's freedom. If there is no scientific means to decide the certainty of different value systems, and if even aesthetic expressions can point the way – since beauty may come from evil and ugliness from sacred spaces – then there is nothing for it but to carry out a supreme act of freedom in order to decide before which god (or devil) one must sacrifice one's intellect. This tragic paradox is part and parcel of the intense melancholy that permeates modernity: freedom becomes a path towards the absurd. This is the spleen of capitalism: industrial society feels a strong elective affinity towards melancholy. Max Weber did not see it in this way: but he suffered it. If he had consulted his much-admired Schiller, he would have discovered a disturbing link between the exaltation of freedom and melancholy, an enthusiasm imbued with romanticism that heralded the paradoxes of modernity, even though in the great dramatist there is no sacrifice of the intellect.

Schiller takes up Kant's views on the sublime to explain that it is a mixed feeling:

> It is a composition of melancholy which at its utmost is manifested in a shudder, and of joyousness which can mount to rapture . . . This combination of two contradictory perceptions in a single feeling demonstrates our moral independence in an irrefutable manner.[60]

Schiller considers that natural objects cannot relate to us in two opposing, distinct ways: as a result, it is we human beings who relate to objects by uniting two diametrically opposed natures. This demonstrates that we enjoy a great demoniacal freedom.[61] As Isaiah Berlin has pointed out, Schiller rejects the Kantian solution, as it seems to him that even though in Kant our will frees us from the laws of nature, it leads us along a narrow path towards an inexorably Calvinist world where mankind is free only to fulfil his duty.[62] This is why the heroes of Schiller's tragedies can be abominable and even satanic, while at the same time incarnating essential truths. These heroes are the proof Weber wished for that something can be valid even when it is not beautiful, sacred or good.

Schiller's melancholy ecstasy allows us to discover mankind's sublime freedom. Modern spleen also pushes human beings towards freedom, but this is a freedom that invites them to sacrifice their intelligence on the altar of ideals. Baudelaire expressed this in a horrifying way in the 'Spleen et idéal' section of *Les Fleurs du mal*. Rather than in the dreadful ennui created by vignette and hospital beauties, Baudelaire finds the flower of his ideal red in the criminal soul of Lady Macbeth or in the strange pose of Night created by Michelangelo.[63] To paraphrase Weber, we have here a sacrifice typical of those negative theologies that aim to approach the sacred by means of a negation of the world and even of divinity itself, which is described as a void, a kind of nothingness.

Weber believes it is impossible to choose between diverse ideals and different systems, between warring gods. However, as if intuiting that his radical relativism leads directly to a devastating anguish when faced with the absurd act of choosing, Weber stealthily introduces the old lifeline offered by Calvinist salvation: 'It is destiny that decides about these gods and their eternal struggle, not "science".' And the 'destiny' of our time is nothing less than the abandonment of the grandiose pathos of the Christian ethic, the disappearance from public life of 'ultimate, most sublime values' and their withdrawal to the spaces of ultra-terrestrial mysticism or the fraternity of close relationships between individuals.[64] It is the advent of pagan polytheism. Thus it is 'destiny' that inexorably leads to disenchantment, which might slightly lessen modern man's anguish since he would be able to accept the superfluous nature of his decisions and choices, in the hope that a force completely beyond him – the destiny of history – will rescue him from the iron cage. The danger is that the cage becomes a culture unified around the *here-and-now*, a culture trapped in *circumstance*, offering no way out to a boundless, free world: because outside the cage . . . there are only more cages. The fateful return to polytheism Weber refers to is the fragmentation of the world into many cages. We are left with the hope that their doors are open, or at least, if they are locked, that we have not lost the keys for ever. In fact, in his 1919 lecture, Weber can find only three ways out, and they all lead to other cages: to cling to the old churches, to set out on a mystical other-worldly journey, or to withdraw to the narrowest circle of community.[65]

I suppose that these three cages could be symbolically linked, in his imagination, to the options represented respectively by his mother, whom he idolized; by the poetry of Rilke, whom he considered a mystic, and by the struggle of Otto Gross, who repelled him. An indication that great values had abandoned public spaces is that in Weber's view the best aesthetic expressions were now produced as intimate art rather than in its monumental forms.

The great monuments are gradually disappearing. All around him, Weber sees a broken world, where disintegration predominates: there are no longer any links between beauty, pleasure, goodness, reason and the sacred. The world is losing the magic that once enveloped it; everywhere there is disenchantment, according to a word Schiller uses that Weber likes, and the capitalist spirit is slipping away, to be replaced by the spleen of capitalism: 'This life is a hospital where every sick person is possessed by the idea of changing beds,' writes Baudelaire in a poem with a significant title in English – 'Anywhere out of the World' (taken from Edgar Allan Poe – which reads like a true declaration of war against the inner-worldly ascetic reason of the puritan ethic.[66] The poet's soul cries to him at the end that it wants to go anywhere, not simply to change beds (or cages) as long as it is out of this world!

Similarly to Kant in his field, Weber was aware of the presence of a world beyond the frontiers of the rational economic order, a territory unknown and unknowable to the capitalist spirit, despite at the same time being dangerously close and intimate. He also suffered vertigo faced with the maelstrom of a sick pagan world filled with pleasures and pains that were completely foreign to the rationality of bourgeois culture. The powerful attraction of this mystical region left its mark on Weber's work, but he almost always succeeded in keeping closed the doors communicating with what the Königsberg philosopher termed a realm of shadows and a paradise of fantasts. Weber was afraid that aesthetic, worldly pleasures would lead him to the dominions of dissolving and subversive pagan ethics. He was no longer confident, as Kant or Schiller had been, that exploring the sublime could help him understand the hospital that the world was becoming. As a result, he felt that sublime, sacred melancholy was turning into a monstrous pagan ennui. In order to understand the encroaching new polytheist disorder, it was a very good idea to use the metaphor of elective affinities. How could one confront the chaos of the links between pleasure and melancholy, between goodness and suffering, the sacred and ugliness, evil and beauty, reason and secularization? Caught up in this disorderly tangle of 'correlations', modern society refuses to submit to a fateful destiny, preferring the fickle rhythms of elective affinities.

These elective affinities weave an immense social network not constructed according to any predetermined idea, not obeying any model or plan, and not predestined to an end fatefully written on the tablets of destiny. And yet the result of the intertwining of countless elective affinities is not a chaotic jumble, but rather a socio-cultural configuration that is both coherent and organized. One of these configurations was identified by Weber as the 'spirit of capitalism'. Although we could find many gaps and errors in his explanation, we have to admit that this is a great sociological discovery achieved thanks to the creative use of the metaphor of elective affinities suggested by Goethe. I would prefer to speak of 'selective affinities': this slight change brings us closer to modern biological ideas of evolution based on a process of natural selection of the most functional or suitable characteristics. In this manner, the metaphor of selective affinities not only helps us to understand the construction of social textures but raises genetic questions about their origin and development.

In general, Max Weber avoided causal genetic explanations that a search for sociological or historical laws might entail. His work *Economy and Society*, for example, is dominated by an obsession for classification that leads him to present lengthy sequences of lists of conceptual definitions of types and categories. His taxonomic enthusiasm led him to elaborate very precise descriptions of certain types of social order, of domination or community, that are still useful to us as exemplary and stimulating conceptual models. His connections and coherences are generally accepted simply as the expression of statistical probabilities. However, this classificatory obsession constantly brings Weber up against the problem of historical and genealogical connections, since every effective system of classification – as Patrick Tort has demonstrated – contains within itself the conditions for its own subversion. This is because the typological or classificatory act itself contains a genealogical principle.[67] One example will suffice to illustrate the point. For Weber, there are only three pure kinds of legitimate domination: the rational, traditional and charismatic. The starting point for his analysis is the most modern form of domination, represented by the Western, bureaucratic, professionalized and formalist kind. The contrast with the traditional and charismatic types contains a tacit question that can be read between the lines: what are the genetic and historical connections between them? In fact, we already know the answer, which appears explicitly in *The Protestant Ethic* or in the lecture on science as a vocation: the final destination is exemplified by the rational, bureaucratic form of domination.

Notwithstanding this, in the genealogy of capitalist domination there also exists something that Weber's rigid typology obscures: a black light emanating from ancient pagan sources.

The legitimacy of modern domination is not entirely based on a formal rationality, but also on the irrational bases of capitalist spleen. Paradoxically, modern capitalism is unable to function without the melancholic aura that surrounds the obsessive and frequently frustrated search for artistic, sensual and moral pleasures initiated by Romanticism, continued by the Modernists and exalted by the major counter-currents of the early years of the twentieth century.

AS I HAVE said, Max Weber was unable to perceive the huge transcendence of the aestheticizing and hedonist spirit unfolding before his eyes. Nor did he grasp the importance of melancholy in the birth of the modern spirit, even though the dreadful illness troubled him greatly. However, we can see that his metaphor of the steel shell refers to an individual caught in a mechanical world dominated by the technological conditions of production, dominated by the desire for profit, secular passions and convulsive arrogance that has lost touch with the ascetic spirit. This modern man, enclosed in his steel shell, is not dissimilar to the man described by Bunyan as living in the darkness of sin in his cage. Both have sinned by yielding to earthly forces and abandoning ancient ideals and beliefs.

In order to escape the deepest depression, of whose threat he was always extremely conscious, Weber was in the habit of applying an effective ascetic formula. As he himself says in a letter to his wife written during the early years of their marriage, he managed to avoid depression 'because I worked constantly and this did not let my nervous system and my brain get any rest'.[68] Following the example of the puritan faithful, he worked stubbornly at his productive worldly tasks to escape from melancholic anxiety. But this proved to be no solution, and in 1898, when he was only 34, Max Weber fell into a state of profound melancholy. He suffered a nervous breakdown, cried a lot, could not work, sought refuge in solitude, and was exhausted by insomnia.[69] He never completely recovered.

In affirming that Max Weber suffered from devastating melancholy I have no intention of carrying out a retrospective psychiatric autopsy. Many years ago, Hans Gerth and C. Wright Mills invited the reader to carry out a psychoanalytic anatomy of the great sociologist when they suggested there was a relationship between his confrontation with his father, the egocentric hedonist who crushed his ascetic mother, and the later guilt the son felt for rejecting him shortly before his death. According to them, Weber's mental illness was a consequence of the weight of his guilt in an Oedipal context, although they also mentioned the existence of hereditary factors and a 'constitutional complaint'.[70] Arthur Mitzman has written a memorable and thought-provoking book in the same Freudian psychoanalytical line.[71] What interests me, however, is placing Weber's melancholy within its historical context in order to examine, based on the cultural experiences of the time, the relation between the psychic illness and the spirit of capitalism. So as to make an initial diagnosis, I will turn to Baudelaire and two psychiatrists for help.

Max Weber read a book by Charles Baudelaire that must have made him think of his own troubles: *Le Spleen de Paris*. Here the French poet described in a disturbing manner the links between modernity and melancholy, capitalist life and ennui, between the expanding industrial city and spleen. It is no coincidence that of all the prose poems that make up *Le Spleen de Paris*, in *Economy and Society* Weber should quote precisely from the one referring to crowds:

What men call love is very small, very limited and very weak compared to that ineffable orgy, that holy prostitution of the soul that gives itself utterly, poetry and charity, to the unforeseen that shows itself, to the stranger passing by.[72]

Weber, who doubtless experienced the temptations of this 'holy prostitution of the soul', interprets it as a strange mystical flight that implies a loving surrender without any rational objective, motivated by the act of surrender itself. Love for its own sake is a mystical form of charity opposed to the rational, organized charity of ascetic religiosity.[73] But Baudelaire exults in losing himself in the crowd and becoming intoxicated in an erotic communion with the modern masses that throng the world: 'Whoever does not know how to people his solitude, does not know either how to be alone in the midst of a busy crowd.'[74]

Max Weber was unable either to people his solitude or to be alone in a crowd. When he fell ill, his solitude was impenetrable, but he could not defend his soul against the public gaze. He had no option but to take flight, to seek in the mountains, the countryside and southern climes a fleeting tranquillity. Weber suffered from the illness that Baudelaire describes: spleen, the ancient hypochondriacal melancholy that adopted the most modern of guises. In one of the prose poems, 'The Generous Gambler', Baudelaire offers a remedy to cure spleen: a pact with Satan. The Devil, through Baudelaire, seems to be talking to Weber and to offer him 'the possibility to alleviate and vanquish, throughout your life, that strange malady of Ennui that is the source of all your illnesses and all your wretched progress'. In exchange for the gambler's soul, Satan offers immense worldly riches, everything a modern capitalist spirit could wish for:

> You will reign over your vulgar fellows; you will be flattered and even adored; silver, gold, diamonds, fairy-tale palaces will seek you out and beg you to accept them, without you making the slightest effort to deserve them.[75]

Weber's ascetic, puritan temperament must have shuddered with horror at these devilish lines that offer the reader a remedy for the cruel sickness, an antidote to that dreadful, venomous monster whose identity – 'C'est l'Ennui!' – Baudelaire reveals in 'Au Lecteur', right at the start of *Les Fleurs du mal* with the warning: 'You, reader, know this delicate monster – hypocrite reader, my fellow – my brother!'[76] Satan explains to the gambler that he has lost his soul in order to lessen the boredom, the ennui:

> you will change nations and countries as often as your fantasy dictates; you will be intoxicated by voluptuousness without ever tiring in charming lands where it is always hot and the women have the fragrance of flowers.[77]

Max Weber experienced none of this. Spleen left him in a dreadful state, practically unable to speak, read, write, walk or sleep. He could not shake off his irritation, and his intellectual paralysis was combined with fits of anger and impatience. As his wife Marianne tells us, he wanted to go to another world, far away, and above all he wanted to stop 'playing at being a professor'.[78] At the onset of his collapse, in the summer of 1898, the doctor ordered a course of hydrotherapy and recommended a stay in a crowded, noisy sanatorium on the shores of Lake Constance, where Weber did physical exercises and patiently accepted the treatments. Although at first he appeared to be improving, a year later all his mental faculties failed him, and he fell into a state of such prostration that he had to be interned in a clinic for the mentally infirm at Urach in the Swabian Alps. There, Weber wrote a text for a psychiatrist in which he described his suffering in great detail; this document, written at some point before the First World War, was kept for several years by Karl Jaspers, who praised the objectivity of the descriptions and the clarity of the self-diagnosis. The text was apparently destroyed by Weber's wife in 1945.[79] The great philosopher and psychiatrist Jaspers was of the opinion that the lost manuscript could be considered a classic of its kind thanks to its sincerity and painstaking approach. In fact, Karl Jaspers himself has left us first drafts of a diagnosis of his friend Weber's mental illness. In a 1932 essay on the sociologist, Jaspers refers very briefly to Weber's 'neurosis'.[80] In some written notes for a lecture (1960–61), Jaspers suggests that Weber's illness helped deepen and illuminate his understanding; he admits that the mental disturbance had internal, constitutional causes, but that it was 'a physically vital neurological illness, not an organic illness but rather a curable, functional one, fluctuating incalculably'. He speculates as to whether 'deep knowledge presumes illness', and suggests a comparison with Kierkegaard, Nietzsche and Hölderlin.[81] Some years later, in a letter to Hannah Arendt dated 29 April 1966, he returns to the comparison with Nietzsche and Kierkegaard's illnesses to explain how they differ. Unlike them, he says, Weber was not a genius, and as for his illness:

> It was neither paralysis nor schizophrenia, but something undiagnosable until now. Elementary, somehow biologically based phases were in his life: highest capacity for work and accomplishment, and then collapse during which he could not even read any more. During the last year of his life, he was in a 'manic' but fully disciplined state of mind – we saw him in Heidelberg two months before his death on the occasion of his last visit . . . This suffering seemed immeasurable. If he had lived, he would probably have collapsed anew.[82]

A year after writing this letter to Arendt, Jaspers learned from Else Jaffé that his friend had lied to him and concealed his love affair with her; this news shocked him so much that he wished to revise his opinion of Max Weber, but had no time to do so. In his letter to Else he asked: 'What happens with a man to whom truth is above everything else?'[83] What happens is that, as John Dreijmanis says, borrowing a phrase from Nietzsche, Max Weber was 'human, all too human'.[84]

We can imagine that the lost diagnosis Weber made of his own illness must have been influenced by what he read, and I would suggest that he turned more to Emil Kräpelin than to Sigmund Freud. Weber took a close interest in Kräpelin, the most influential psychiatrist of his day, whom he must surely have met in Heidelberg. He read his work carefully when in 1908 he began research into the psycho-physics of the industrial world, as he wanted to use the psychological findings in both his studies on the weavers in the textile mills and on the sociology of mass phenomena.[85] It is likely that Weber was also interested in applying to his own personal situation Kräpelin's famous treatise on psychiatry, which grew in successive editions until it resulted (from the 1899 edition on) in his influential theory on manic-depressive illness as one single sickness that included different states. How would Doctor Kräpelin have diagnosed Weber's psychic problems? If we take Jaspers's brief comments as a starting point, we might suppose that, having dismissed paranoia, early dementia or schizophrenia, he could have diagnosed a manic-depressive psychosis. What is interesting and original in Kräpelin's definition is that he considered a wide variety of melancholic and maniacal disorders as part of a single illness. However, Kräpelin divided the illness into three main groups: manic, depressive and mixed states. In Weber's case he would have rejected the extreme forms of the illness such as raving madness, paranoid melancholy or manic stupor; instead, I would venture to suggest, he would have spoken of a depressive state he termed *melancholia simplex*, accompanied by occasional lapses into some more serious mixed states. Simple melancholy is defined by Kräpelin as a psychic inhibition without any pronounced hallucinations or delusions:

Thinking is difficult to the patient, a disorder, which he describes in the most varied phrases. He cannot collect his thoughts or pull himself together; his thoughts are as if paralysed, they are immobile. His head feels heavy, quite stupid, as if a board were pushed in front of it, everything is confused. He is no longer able to perceive, or to follow the train of thought of a book or a conversation, he feels weary, enervated, inattentive, inwardly empty; he has no memory, he has no longer command of knowledge formerly familiar to him, he must consider a long time about simple things, he calculates wrongly, makes contradictory statements, does not find words, cannot construct sentences correctly. At the same time complaints are heard that the patient must meditate so much, that fresh thoughts are always coming to him, that he has too much in his head, that he finds no rest, is confused.[86]

Doctor Kräpelin would have thought that at other moments Weber was prey to a kind of hypomania that the French call '*folie raisonnante*', characterized by increases in psychic activity, excitement, exaltation, a greater capacity for work and good humour. Exuberance betrays the underlying illness, which leads to emotional irritation and a lack of satisfaction.[87]

Manic-depressive psychosis was seen by Kräpelin as an illness independent of external influences, whose deep-seated cause is a permanent sick tendency that does not go away in the intervals between attacks. Unlike with Baudelaire's spleen, here there is no chance of turning to the Devil for help. Kräpelin defines four 'fundamental states' which he describes as 'temperaments': the depressive, manic, irritable and cyclotimic. Weber would doubtless have been classified as suffering from an irritable temperament, an underlying and inescapable illness that could only be relieved but never cured. Weber's wife mentions hydrotherapy and the use of a sedative, trional, which is also recommended by Kräpelin, together with others (veronal, luminal, paraldehyde). He suggests large doses of bromide (between 12 and 15 g daily), hypnotics, the avoidance of emotional stimuli, nocturnal cold showers, opium, bed rest, a diet of easily digested foods and hospitalization.[88]

But Weber's melancholy, like the burden of original sin, could not be eradicated, only alleviated. Kräpelin stresses the religious tensions suffered by the manic-depressive, some of whom believe 'everything is enchanted' and feel the influence of the devil as well as the weight of guilt. Kräpelin's description is full of echoes of the seventeenth-century puritans:

> The patient is a great sinner, cannot pray anymore, has forgotten the ten commandments, the creed, the benediction, has lost eternal bliss, has committed the sin against the Holy Ghost, has trafficked in divine things, has not offered enough candles. He has apostatized from God, is gripped firmly by Satan, must do penance.[89]

Karl Jaspers, Weber's friend and admirer, also alluded to the feelings of sin that for him were characteristic of what he called *pure depression*. I do not know if this is applicable to Weber's illness, but undoubtedly it is related, as I have pointed out, to the puritans' exacerbated sense of guilt. In addition, it is interesting to note that Jaspers, in his voluminous *General Psychopathology*, uses the Weberian theory of ideal types to describe the distinction between mania and depression. I have already mentioned this in relation to the manic, although controlled, state his friend suffered in his final days. Weber's depressive collapses could perhaps fit Jaspers's description of the ideal type of depression:

> Its central core is formed from an equally unmotivated and profound sadness to which is added a retardation of psychic events, which is subjectively painful as it is objectively visible. All instinctual activities are subjected to it. The patient does not want to do anything . . . They feel profound

gloom as a sensation in the chest or body. The depth of their melancholy makes them see the world as grim and gray. They look for the unfavorable and unhappy elements of everything.[90]

Throughout his life, Weber was threatened by melancholy, even though he never lost his characteristic determination and lucidity. Whether as sublime Baudelairian spleen or prosaic Kräpelinesque depression, he always felt the influence of the black humour. Intense work unsettled him but he insisted on always returning to his strict intellectual routines. In 1920, the last year of his life, his sister Lili committed suicide, leaving four orphan children whom Weber and his wife decided to adopt. But the combination of the emotions aroused by this suddenly acquired paternity and the intensity of his intellectual efforts yet again produced extreme nervous exhaustion. To friends alarmed by his appearance, Weber confessed that 'the machine wouldn't work anymore', that he had lain stretched out on a sofa, unable to work, overwhelmed by thoughts of death. His wife was absent, but his friend Else Jaffé had comforted him; when she felt he had fallen into the deep pit of melancholy, she commented: 'It was as if a cold hand had touched you.' He replied seriously: 'Yes, Else, that's how it was.' Without a doubt this was the icy hand of the angel of melancholy. Weber's wife, who relates this conversation, immediately afterwards describes an odd romantic scene where on a moonlit night her husband, sitting on the banks of the Isar, contemplates the rapid succession of waves and says softly: 'Yes, that's the way it is; one quickly follows another, but the stream is always the same.' Marianne Weber adds with tender sadness: 'Not what he said, but his tone of voice suggested that ultimate secrets had been unveiled to him for a moment.'[91] Did Weber think that the eternal flow of waves was as much to be feared as spleen?

A few weeks later, in June 1920, the wave of a devastating pneumonia drowned Max Weber forever in the stream.

Benjamin and Ennui

Angels (they say) are often unaware
if they move among living or dead. The eternal current
flows between the two realms, sweeping with it all ages,
and covers them with its roar.
In the end, those who died early have no need of us.
Weaned gently off earthly things as our lips
leave the maternal breast. But we
who need such great mysteries, we for whom
blessed progress is often born of mourning,
Could we live without them?
Rainer Maria Rilke, 'First Duino Elegy'[1]

The flap of a butterfly's wing in the Pyrenees – or so those meteorologists interested in chaos theory think – can produce such a series of effects that a long while later it eventually produces a storm over the River Main. We might also imagine that when a professor blinks on reading a difficult text in Frankfurt he paves the way for a succession of events that culminates, fifteen years later, in the suicide of a philosopher in the Pyrenees. Walter Benjamin, the German philosopher who took his own life in the Pyrenees, would doubtless have been attracted by this idea. And he would have been attracted to it because he was deeply interested in problems of destiny and predicting the future. Once, in 1918, Benjamin insisted to his friend Gershom Scholem: 'A philosophy that does not include the possibility of soothsaying from coffee grounds and cannot explicate it cannot be a true philosophy.'[2]

This affirmation is to be seen in the context of the *Programme of the Coming Philosophy*, a text in which Benjamin aims to extend the Kantian notion of experience to include science, metaphysics and religion. As Gershom Scholem remarked, this would also entail the inclusion of mantic disciplines.

Some years later, in 1925, Walter Benjamin finished the manuscript of his famous study on German Baroque mournful drama. He wanted to present it as a 'Habilitation' thesis at Frankfurt University in order to formally begin a university career. Professor Franz Schultz, who had given him hopes in this respect, was the first to blink when faced with Benjamin's text. He decided to pass it on to the 'aesthetics' department. Professor Schultz, an insignificant intellectual mediocrity, as Benjamin described him in a letter,[3] was afraid that this disturbing student from Berlin would cast a shadow over him. Benjamin's thesis was sent to Professor Hans Cornelius, who unfortunately for him has gone down in the annals of history because Lenin made fun of him in *Materialism and Empiriocriticism* (1909), where he perhaps unjustly described him as a 'policeman with a university chair'.[4] Professor Cornelius also blinked when faced with a text which, he claimed, he could not understand. He therefore asked Benjamin to send him an outline, which he passed on for a decision to his assistant, Doctor Max Horkheimer, who must also have blinked and replied that he was unable to follow Benjamin's argument.[5] Faced with this dispiriting attitude, Benjamin withdrew his submission for the Habilitation, in order to avoid a formal rejection. That was the end of his academic career, and apparently set the seal on his tragic fate: for the next fifteen years he experienced great economic hardship, the break-up of his marriage, and wandered aimlessly around Europe, writing disturbing, fragmentary texts, scraping a living from journalism and fleeing the Nazis but failing to discover an escape route. In the end, cornered in the south of France, he committed suicide in Portbou in September 1940.

Walter Benjamin himself believed that 'he had come into the world under the sign of Saturn', the slow, melancholy star of delays and detours.[6] Many of those who have written about him, from Hannah Arendt to Susan Sontag, have thought he was marked by his saturnine character.[7] In 1921, some years prior to his failed attempt to embark on a university career, Benjamin published an interesting essay on fate and character. In it, he begins by examining the common view, which is so determinist that Laplace himself could have supported it: if we were able on the one hand to know all the components of a person's character and on the other hand were able to determine all the cosmic alignments related to that individual, his entire future could be predicted. We would therefore be able to predict his fate. Laplace had said that an intelligence capable of knowing all the forces driving nature, as well as the respective situation of the beings in it, and which also possessed a sufficiently vast power of analysis, would be able to include in the same formula the movements of both the largest bodies of the cosmos as well as those of the lightest atoms. For such an intelligence, no uncertainty would exist, and both future and past would be plainly visible. The human spirit, Laplace added, offers a small example of this intelligence in the perfect way it has modelled astronomy.[8] For his part Benjamin, who was more attracted to esotericism than astronomy, observes that those modern spirits who are willing to accept the interpretation of character based on people's physical features nonetheless reject the idea that their fate can be known from the lines in their hands. This is absurd, Benjamin argues, because those who believe they can predict the fate of human beings think that the future is somehow already present and accessible, in the same way as a person's character is. But both fate and character reveal themselves through signs, rather than showing themselves directly. Obviously, there is no causal relationship between signs and signified. Fate is not immediately present: what exists is a system of signs that has to be interpreted.[9] When Benjamin saw the astounded blink of Professor Schultz's eyes, that sign allowed him to understand that his academic future was doomed to failure: but could it have led him to think it would lead to his own suicide fifteen years later?

In reality, the 'butterfly effect' that the blink of an academic's eye can cause is an image of contingency, employed to demonstrate that it is *impossible* to predict the future development of a dynamic system such as the climate. The 'butterfly effect' referred to by those people interested in chaos theory is a metaphor related to the dependency that stems from the starting point of certain dynamic systems: a tiny variation of conditions at a certain moment produces very different effects to those which would have occurred if that initial disturbance had not taken place. However, it is important to point out that this starting point, like the flap of a butterfly's wing, *is not the cause* of the storm on the River Main.[10] To understand what happens in these systems, the model of so-called 'strange attractors' is used; their strangeness comes from the fact that they reconcile two apparently contradictory effects: on the one hand they attract events to the nearby trajectories that converge on them; on the other they are dependent in a way that arises from their starting point. This situation is typical, for example, of the evolution of a cloud in the sky: anybody can recognize its strange shape because it contains, we might say, a phenomenon of the attraction of trajectories; yet it is impossible to foresee the shape or position of the cloud only a few minutes after the first observation. The same thing happens with the smoke rising from a cigarette: while it is easy to recognize the column of smoke as it rises, it is impossible to predict the turbulent shape of its dissipation. In a fascinating book, the mathematician David Ruelle explains that the position of a planet (let us say Saturn) at any particular moment (let us say 15 July 1892, the day Benjamin was born) appears to be independent with regard to the state of the weather in the Pyrenees, and therefore of the philosopher's frame of mind at the moment when he took his life. Astrologists, however, would deny that these facts are independent . . . Ruelle says that the two are certainly not independent, since the weather responds to its starting point, however remote and imperceptible that may be: so here, the position of Saturn corresponds to the flap of the butterfly's wings, which over the course of time leads to important consequences, even if these are unpredictable (something astrologers would not accept). Ruelle says it is very difficult to provide a mathematical explanation for this situation, which combines independence and dependence: in other words, independence with regard to any calculation of probabilities but at the same time dependence that arises from the starting point.[11]

In his essay, Benjamin follows a parallel path: the supposition is false – he maintains – that by knowing all the inner and outer details of a character we are able to determine that person's fate. If such were the case, character and fate would coincide, and therefore Nietzsche's saying would be applicable: 'If a man has character, he has an experience that constantly recurs.'[12] Benjamin concludes that if there is character, then fate is constant: and that therefore *there is no fate*. It is as if the weather repeated itself exactly the same each year, or if every time we light a cigarette, the rising column of smoke dissipates in exactly the same way. And so Benjamin resolves to make a clear distinction between character and destiny. He also maintains that it is a mistake to link destiny with guilt, sin and therefore with morality. Nor should it be related to innocence. The idea of fate is incarnated in tragedy and in the law, when it appears as a life that is *first of all* condemned and then *later on* seen as guilty. This is why a judge can see fate wherever he chooses: each time he pronounces a sentence he must at the same time decide a fate. The law in fact does not condemn punishment: it condemns sin and guilt. Benjamin is categorical: 'fate is the guilt context of the living.'[13]

Moreover, for Benjamin character is not a net or fabric that becomes increasingly dense until it creates a cloth in which the good and bad qualities of a person can be seen. Just as fate is incarnated in tragedy, so character is to be found in comedy. Here, character does not express a dense, complex moral fabric, but the comic hero is portrayed with one simple trait that illuminates the entire character. In Molière, miserliness or hypochondria do not represent twisted ethical complexities or infinite psychological complications. Unlike the labyrinth of guilt that traps the tragic hero, the protagonist of the comedy of character – in his natural innocence – is free and simple, and escapes from the universe of original guilt. But modern mantic practices unfruitfully associate the signs of character with moral values. By contrast, Benjamin believes that the ancient and medieval physiognomists were more lucid when they recognized that character can only be understood thanks to a few basic concepts that are morally indifferent, such as those established by the theory of temperaments.

If any visionary angel, of the new breed that Benjamin liked to invoke, had visited him in 1925 and interpreted the signs and the blinking eyes in his academic and political environment, he would doubtless have immediately called on the angelic chorus to start the mourning process for the fateful end met by the philosopher. Rilke had already declared: 'All angels are terrible.'[14] That angel would without doubt have known if the mourning was a result of the melancholy temperament predominant in Benjamin's character or rather due to a fate sealed by the context of guilt that condemned the philosopher. As Bernd Witte has pointed out, Benjamin took the figure of the Angelus Novus as a secret symbol of his own project as a critical writer: an angel who could decode the chaotic fragments of recent history.[15] The *Angelus Novus* – referring both to a watercolour by Paul Klee that Benjamin had bought and to a journal which in the end was never published – refers to a Talmudic legend which says that new angels are being created all the time, but that they, after singing their hymn to God, immediately dissolve into nothingness. I should like to believe that these angelic hosts helped Walter Benjamin recognize the ruins and disorder of modern life and to survive in the face of disaster. Irrational spaces held a great fascination for Benjamin, who, however, covered them with a headstone of melancholy. Around it, the angels of modernity perform their mourning rites in order to dispel the dangers that threaten out of chaos. Some of them are enlightened angels who want to advance like a scientific army against the shadows of disorder. But others, the angels of melancholy, are there to remind the first angels, the enlightenend ones, that they will never be able to illuminate or conquer all the territory.

WALTER BENJAMIN'S THOUGHT appears to oscillate between the chaos that hovers around melancholy characters threatened by ennui and the order imposed by a tragic fate. This latter idea predominates in his lengthy essay on Goethe's *Elective Affinities* published in 1925, that fateful year that was a turning point for our philosopher. Goethe's novel introduces the problem of the tragic consequences brought about by the choice of certain erotic affinities that subvert the established moral order. Benjamin believes that the plot of the novel is dominated by the mythical idea of a fate that leads the characters to their ruin. There is no ethical conundrum that the protagonists have to face when they have to choose whether or not they allow themselves to be attracted by outside affinities, but rather the idea of 'an order whose members live out their lives under a nameless law, a fatality that fills their world with the pallid light of a solar eclipse'.[16] Unlike Max Weber, Benjamin is not interested in the subtlety of human relationships influenced by elective affinities. He prefers to stress the determinism that condemns the actors to an inexorable fate. Of course, one has to remember that Benjamin is talking of fictional characters in a novel, not real human beings. That is why he refuses to submit the characters to any ethical judgements.[17] However, we might suppose that Benjamin is not merely writing a critical study of a literary text, but is also referring to both contemporary social life and even to his own personal circumstances. During the period when he was writing the essay, his marriage was being dissolved, and both he and his wife had chosen to initiate other erotic relationships.[18] He also alludes to Goethe's life, seeing him as an example of how 'the human being petrifies in the chaos of symbols and loses the freedom unknown to the ancients.'[19] Right from the beginning of the essay, thanks to a quotation from Klopstock, Benjamin affirms that blind choices lead to sacrifice. Choices made through affinities that break the established norms are 'blind' and inevitably lead to disaster. A disastrous end that is presented as a mythical archetype of sacrifice, in which the 'victim of destiny', Ottilie, is in fact innocent: but her death opens the way for the expiation of the guilty ones.[20] Freedom of choice is nothing more than a semblance: 'it is the chimerical striving for freedom that draws down fate on the characters in the novel.'[21]

To Walter Benjamin, the world of the *Elective Affinities* is a grey, demoniacal and saturnine place, ruled by an anguish regarding death and ennui in the face of a constantly repeated destiny: 'the Eternal Return of the Same, as it stonily prevails over the most intimately varied feelings, is the sign of fate, whether it is self-identical in the life of many or repeats itself in the individual.'[22] To grasp the importance that Benjamin gave to the association between ennui and the eternal return, we can read the entries in a section from his *Arcades Project*, 'Convolute D', devoted to precisely these two concepts. Moreover, from the outset Benjamin refers to the weather, that cosmic force about which weak, frail people love to speculate. It is symptomatic that what the philosopher considers the most 'intimate and mysterious topic', the influence of the weather/climate on human beings, should have become a topic for superficial conversation:

> Nothing bores the ordinary man more than the cosmos.
> Hence, for him, the deepest connection between weather
> and boredom. How fine the ironic overcoming of this

attitude in the story of the splenetic Englishman who wakes up one morning and shoots himself because it is raining. Or Goethe: how he managed to illuminate the weather in his meteorological studies, so that one is tempted to say he undertook this work solely in order to be able to integrate even the weather into his waking, creative life.[23]

Paris's rainy climate is paradigmatic, and Benjamin uses a quotation from Balzac to link it to the commercial passages the French built in imitation of the covered arcades of Milan and Naples.[24] All this reminds him of the Surrealist painting of Giorgio de Chirico, who once said of Paris: 'It is only here that it is possible to paint. The streets have so many shades of grey.'[25] It seems to me that if we wish to find an image of the boring world of the elective affinities as Benjamin saw it, we ought to contemplate de Chirico's metaphysical paintings: *Melanconia* (1912), *La Mélancolie d'une belle journée* (1913) or *Mystère et mélancolie d'une rue* (1912). It is interesting to note that de Chirico suffered from melancholy, as he himself tells us in his memoirs. He also explains the influence of Nietzsche on his work: he relates that in Florence, around 1910, he was painting very little and reading a lot:

above all, I read philosophy books and was prey to severe crises of melancholy . . . my Boecklin period was over, and I had begun to paint pictures in which I tried to express that mysterious and powerful feeling I had discovered in the books of Nietzsche: the melancholy of fine autumn days, evenings in Italian cities. This was the prelude to the *Squares of Italy* that I painted a short while later in Paris, and later in Milan, Florence and Rome.[26]

De Chirico's cityscapes represent a petrified, unmoving life, like an empty still-life that is completely indifferent and eternally repeats the same twilight shadows, the same arches, the same mysterious statue of melancholy, in a senseless, boring wait. This is the mythical circle that Nietzsche describes, as quoted by Benjamin: 'existence as it is, without meaning or aim, yet recurring inevitably without any finale into nothingness: the eternal return'.[27]

In *Elective Affinities*, Goethe uses a metaphor taken from the natural sciences to suggest that in free choices there also exists the influence of an order which is expressed in a kind of language used by nature. He took this idea from a work by the Swedish chemist Torberg Bergmann, entitled *De atractionibus electivis* (1775), published in German in 1782 as *Die Wahlverwandtschaften*, exactly the same title as Goethe's novel.[28] In Chapter XII of this work, Goethe could find an example almost identical to the one he uses in his novel: the Swedish chemist cites the combination of 'vitriolic' (sulphuric) acid with 'natural alkali' to produce the calcareous bases for gypsum. Goethe took something else from Bergmann: the use of letters to denote chemical substances (A, B, C, a, b, c). This alphabet allows him to understand the language of nature and to decipher the codes explaining the elective affinities. Benjamin did not concur with any of this. For him, nature is mute, and this leads him to affirm the metaphysical truth according to which the whole of nature would protest if it were lent a language: 'Because she is mute, nature mourns. Yet the inversion of this proposition leads even further into the essence of nature; the sadness of nature makes her mute'.[29]

What protagonist, what character, could survive in the grey world doomed to a tragic fate, where society makes all choice pointless and where nature is in mourning? As an experiment, I should like to introduce a character whom Benjamin placed at the centre of modern life: the *flâneur*, a creation of the city of Paris. This character is born into the urban labyrinth and grows up as a tireless passer-by who plunges into the modern order with his erratic, contingent and adventurous behaviour. The *flâneur* knows how to confront fateful destiny by means of the uncertainty of his walking, which has no intent or aim but which allows him to contemplate his surroundings and buildings with insatiable curiosity. And yet, Benjamin believes, the stroller behaves in the same way as goods in capitalist society: 'the labyrinth is the right path for the person who always arrives early enough at his destination. This destination is the marketplace.'[30] In his wandering, the *flâneur* finds a way to escape from ennui and spleen, and in doing so becomes a character who is extremely resistant to the rainy climate, the greyness of the world, astrological predictions, the irrationality of actions or choices, the eternal return of the same. Chaos and order have little effect on him ... 'the labyrinth is the habitat of the dawdler. The path followed by someone reluctant to reach his goal becomes labyrinthine.'[31] For Benjamin, the *flâneur* has nothing in common with philosophical walks like those that the protagonists of *Elective Affinities* undertake, or the heroes of Romantic thought. The *flâneur*, on the contrary, is like 'a werewolf wandering through the social jungle', as Edgar Allan Poe described him in *The Man of the Crowd*.[32]

Of course, we could say that in the end the strange wanderings of a *flâneur* guided solely by his chance curiosity is still subject to the divine intentions that seal his destiny. Chance would simply be our ignorance of fate, or what amounts to the same thing, our inability to appreciate and reproduce every detail of the development of a social (or natural) process. We know, for example, that the way we throw dice determines their outcome. If we were able to throw the dice in exactly the same way a second time – as if we were gods – we would obtain identical results. But, as in the butterfly effect, the slightest change in the throwing of the dice produces consequences that alter the result. We could possibly imagine that there is a profound, radical chance governing the behaviour of our *flâneur* in his strolling around Paris: in that case there could be no possibility of 'the same' even a second time (and still less in an eternally repeated manner). As an ironic aside, we might here recall the famous remark Einstein made when he affirmed – regarding quantum theory – that the Good Lord does not roll dice; to which Niels Bohr retorted: 'Don't suggest to God what He should do.' Without a doubt the fundamental indecisiveness of the *flâneur* brings a new dimension that can disrupt the force of destiny and guilt. Benjamin himself appears to intuit this when he writes:

> Just as waiting seems to be the proper state of the impassive thinker, doubt appears to be that of the flâneur. An elegy by Schiller contains the phrase: 'the hesitant wing of the butterfly'. This points to that association of wingedness with the feeling of indecision which is so characteristic of hashish intoxication.[33]

This, however, was only a hallucinatory, fleeting illumination, possibly when Benjamin recalled the strange, liberating sensations that hashish produced in him. It was the apparition of the angel of corrosive doubt that for a few brief moments nourished the hope he might escape his fate. In some travel recollections published in 1928 as part of a book with the significant title *One-way Street*, there is a curious note on the angel of hope by Andrea Pisano, which Benjamin saw on the portal of the baptistery in Florence: the *Spes* is 'sitting, she helplessly extends her arms toward a fruit that remains beyond her reach. And yet she is winged. Nothing is more true.'[34] What is true? Why doesn't the angel of hope fly to reach the desired fruit? It must be indecision that is paralysing him . . . or the intoxicating effects of hashish. And yet, by contrast to a boring wait, doubt stimulates the *flâneur* to carry on walking without a goal. Does Benjamin launch him into the one-way street of fateful destiny? It is as if life were a rope attached to the tree of death. When we shake it, the rope takes on a variety of shapes, and always seems like a path irremediably leading us to our final destiny. In despair, some use the rope to hang themselves with from the tree. Others stretch it to try to lengthen or even snap it. Still others make the rope describe a complicated labyrinth or fill it with knots. The rope can also be used to make strange hieroglyphs. It is as though the rope is fate, and that its loops, knots, tensions and tangles constitute character. In one of his final texts, *Central Park*, Benjamin asserted: 'For people as they are now, there is only one radical novelty – and always the same one: death.'[35]

In 1925, Walter Benjamin could apparently have chosen at least four different paths towards death. Each of these possible futures could be symbolized by the name of a city, as if they were four allegorical labyrinths: Frankfurt, Jerusalem, Moscow and Paris. I have already mentioned the first path: Benjamin wished to be recognized as an academic at Frankfurt University; we can imagine that he would have become a prominent and active member of the school of philosophy led by Theodor Adorno, Max Horkheimer, Leo Löwenthal and Herbert Marcuse at the Institute of Social Research, which was transferred to New York with the outbreak of the Second World War. This path was closed to him when his Habilitation thesis was rejected, although years later he was sup-ported by the Institute and had the opportunity, which he could not take, of travelling to New York at Adorno's invitation.

Another path that opened for Benjamin was, as his friend Scholem says: 'a career and a future in the bosom of Judaism.'[36] This path led to Jerusalem, where the university had not only invited him but had helped by paying his fees in advance. Around 1927, Benjamin seemed determined to travel to Palestine, and even studied Hebrew to prepare himself for integrating into Jewish society. Of course, this alternative meant much more than a post as an academic at Jerusalem University: it implied his immersion in the Jewish messianic tradition that so appealed to him, and an encounter with his religious roots. This journey had been fervently promoted by his friend Scholem, who wrote a moving account of how the project failed since it clashed with other alternatives.[37] On 6 June 1929 Benjamin confessed to his friend that the idea of travelling to Jerusalem came up against 'a pathological vacillation which, I am sorry to say, I have already noticed in myself from time to time.'[38]

Scholem was well aware that, as well as this existential doubt, there existed another alternative that got in the way of the journey to Palestine: this was the great attraction Benjamin felt for Marxism and the revolutionary light shining from Moscow. As is well known, this attraction was linked to Benjamin's love for Asja Lacis, a Lithuanian Bolshevik who had a powerful influence on Benjamin and who encouraged his relationship with Bertolt Brecht. Benjamin travelled to Moscow in December 1926 to visit her, and stayed for a couple of months (she had been interned in a sanatorium following a nervous breakdown). Some time later, Asja Lacis began trying to arrange for Benjamin to emigrate to the Soviet Union; these plans came to naught, as did his relationship with Asja.[39] The Marxist influence persisted, although it produced the strangest fruits.

The path that won out was a different one. In a 1929 letter to Scholem, Benjamin explains that his trip to Jerusalem is facing several difficulties, chief among which lies in the situation 'that preliminary studies for – not yet, by any means, work on – the *Paris Arcades* cannot be interrupted at this moment'.[40] This project, conceived in 1924 and begun in 1927, meant that Benjamin's erratic life revolved around Paris. The Parisian labyrinth ended by attracting him in 1933, when he escaped from Nazi Germany. Possibly without realizing it, he chose the path of the *flâneur*.

BENJAMIN'S STUDY OF the Lutheran playwrights of the German Baroque period opened the door on a much more desolate and desperate world than the one Goethe presented in *Elective Affinities*.

In its outright denial that 'good works' can miraculously change the spiritual order imposed by destiny, Lutheranism, according to Benjamin, inculcated in the people an extraordinary discipline and an obedient attitude: 'but in its great men it produced melancholy,' including in Luther himself.[41] What Benjamin was searching for in the world of elective affinities, without ever completely finding it, he discovered in all its gloomy splendour in the German *Trauerspiel*: melancholy. In an excellent study that reveals great insight, Max Pensky has demonstrated the central importance of the theme of melancholy in Walter Benjamin's thought.[42] This not only involves the brilliant historical and literary dissection of a fundamental problem in Baroque culture, but demonstrates Benjamin's audacious creative appropriation of a melancholy vision that he unearths from the ruins of a little-known and poorly appreciated dramaturgy: the seventeenth-century *Trauerspiel*. Benjamin's study, which was his frustrated Habilitation thesis, was published in book form in Berlin in January 1928.

The preliminary chapter, described by George Steiner as one of the most impenetrable pieces of prose ever written in a modern language, was without a doubt the reason for the fateful blinking of the eyes of Benjamin's professors. It can be interpreted in many ways, but we cannot fail to see in it a challenge: the work is presented as a tearing apart, as the drilling of a well that allows us to plunge into the depths of the Baroque state of mind.[43] Benjamin feels vertigo, and even warns of the danger of bringing into our own time a spiritual world full of contradictions. Why might it be dangerous? Because Benjamin was determined to delve deep into Baroque melancholy and to pour it over his own life.

Lutheranism, Benjamin believes, displayed a pagan Germanic element in its obscure belief in subjection to fate: 'Human actions were deprived of all value. Something new arose: an empty world.'[44] Ordinary people responded to this void by simple attitudes of faith, but more complex spirits found themselves enveloped in a *tedium*

vitae and a strange state of mind: mourning for the fall of human-
kind, the huge collapse that swept away the whole of nature, which
fell silent and sank into sadness.[45] Mourning is a feeling which
restores life to the empty world by placing a mask on it. Thanks to
this, the melancholy person can contemplate the world and feel an
enigmatic satisfaction.[46] This is where the essence of German
Baroque theatre known as *Trauerspiel* resides. It is the mourning
or grief (*Trauer*) which gives this kind of theatre its peculiar character and distinguishes it from tragedy. It concerns a mournful
drama that refers to history and a desolate world of sad, indecisive
monarchs who are both ostentatious and apathetic: tragedy by contrast is rooted in a mythical dimension, as is the case in the world of
elective affinities depicted by Goethe. Unlike Max Weber, Benjamin
had a clear understanding of the melancholy repercussions of
Lutheran ethics.

The mask that the poets and playwrights put on the world in
mourning for cosmic abandonment is made up of an enigmatic
collection, almost cabbalistic in nature, of symbols, allegories,
emblems and hieroglyphs. The melancholy gaze contemplates a
world of inert objects that lie dead all around the allegorist:

> If the object becomes allegorical under the gaze of melan-
> choly, if melancholy causes life to flow out of it and it
> remains dead but eternally secure, then it is exposed to the
> allegorist, it is unconditionally in his power.[47]

This view has been interpreted by Susan Buck-Morss as a critique
of Baroque allegory, which Benjamin saw as an idealist illusion.
Apparently, this critique was later distilled in *The Arcades Project*,
which she sees as a Marxist reworking of the philosophical method
employed in the essay on German funereal drama.[48] This interpretation is not obvious, and according to Buck-Morss, the unwary
reader will not be able to see it: one has to decode Benjamin's text as

she does in order to perceive its true meaning. However, this decoding does not convince Max Pensky, who suspects that those critical texts by Benjamin that analyse Baroque melancholy are themselves melancholic.[49] He is surely right: Benjamin sees the theory of melancholy as a powerful 'dialectic of Saturn' which has led to abundant accurate anthropological intuitions and which 'endows the soul, on the one hand, with sloth and dullness, on the other, with the power of intelligence and contemplation'.[50] Of course, Benjamin's critical reflection is by no means a despairing collapse into subjectivity. There is something that puts a brake on his fall: possibly the fact that, as Theodor Adorno has suggested, he finds in mourning the ultimate revolutionary category, that of redemption.[51] The melancholy gaze deprives objects of life by converting them into allegories. In dying, the object no longer gives off its own sense or meaning. Now it is the allegorist who gives it meaning, who traces a sign that transforms the object into something different.[52] Benjamin in turn builds an allegorical construction in his book on tragic drama. The puzzle comes from trying to establish whether Benjamin *assigns* meanings to his discoveries or simply *finds* them and *deciphers* them. Max Pensky tends towards the latter;[53] Bernd Witte on the other hand believes that the conclusions of Benjamin's essay represent a movement towards metaphysics.[54] On reading Benjamin's text, I have the impression that the melancholy allegorist has cast his subjectivity into the void, the abyss. But at this point theology intervenes miraculously to rescue it: 'Subjectivity, like an angel falling into the depths, is brought back by allegories, and is held fast in Heaven, in God, by "mysterious ponderation".' This mysterious contemplation signifies, according to Benjamin, the balancing intervention of the divinity in the work of art.[55] This angel of subjective melancholy is similar to those that appear in Baroque sculptural decoration: dangerously hanging in mid-air, they appear to be sustained by supernatural forces. I shall return to this strange, mysterious contemplation later in this chapter.

Even though Benjamin was aware of the great limitations of the Baroque playwrights' melancholy gaze, this did not prevent him from grasping the notion that melancholy, as an expectation of the Messiah, expressed the theological promise of redemption of the world, and becomes a model of hope, as Pensky points out, inspired by an essay Adorno wrote on Kierkegaard. There must be a heroic melancholy that could be described by Adorno's beautiful image: the bitter tears in the eyes of a reader trying with great difficulty to solve a riddle provide him with the optic he needs to decipher signs of redemption in the text of the world.

When he dealt with these same topics in his famous text *Mourning and Melancholy* of 1915, Sigmund Freud's view was very different. According to his interpretation, the loss of the beloved object produces anger that the subject directs against himself. The melancholy subject, instead of directing his reproaches and hatred towards the erotic object that has abandoned him, turns his rancour against his own ego in a painful process of demolition and destruction. Freud's interpretation radically contrasts with the European tradition, picked up by Walter Benjamin, which associates the sadness felt at the loss of the desired object with the creation of the melancholy subject, who discovers in his pain the strength needed for intellectual and artistic creation. The cultural history of melancholy contradicts Freud's idea: the sad task of melancholic mourning, despite its huge dangers, can strengthen the creator and the artist's ego. Of course, clinical experience supports Freud: whereas in mourning the world appears as an impoverished desert, in melancholy it is the ego that appears as empty, worthless and despicable.

Freud uses Prince Hamlet as an example: a sick person who degrades himself and sees himself as a person riddled with defects.[56] By contrast, Benjamin considers Hamlet as the foremost example of the Renaissance tradition that is able to discover in melancholy 'the reflection of a distant light, shining back from the depths of self-absorption', since only in a princely life 'is melancholy redeemed, by being confronted by himself'.[57] His interpretation coincides with that of Victor Hugo, who had seen in the 'pallid hesitation' and in the 'grandiose pallor' of Hamlet's soul the same melancholy that Dürer had portrayed in his angel: Hamlet also has

> above his head the eviscerated bat and, at his feet, science, the globe, the compass, the hourglass, love and on the horizon behind him a huge, terrible sun that seems to make the sky even darker.[58]

Freud admits that the melancholy person could be right and be able to perceive the truth more clearly than those who are not melancholic. Self-criticism could bring the subject closer to self-awareness, to the discovery of his own insignificance, his lack of originality, his egotism or his dishonesty. Freud wonders why it was necessary to suffer from melancholy to discover these truths.[59] Benjamin probably did not know Freud's text, but it would have proved useful to him when he confronted melancholy in its most devalued forms. In 1931 Benjamin published a bad-tempered, poisonous critique of the 'tormented stupidity' of some writers, which with acid irony he defines as the most recent metamorphosis of melancholy in its two-thousand-year history. This is the 'left-wing melancholy' typical of those intellectuals whom Benjamin scorns as radical publicists who are nothing more than a 'decadent bourgeois imitation of the proletariat'. Benjamin's text could be the cruel result of having placed the writers he criticizes – principally Erich Kästner – on the psychoanalyst's couch, and discovering that what these tortured left-wing melancholics in fact are showing is 'the affliction of replete men who can no longer devote all their money to their stomachs' and whose fatalist rumblings 'have more to do with flatulence than with subversion', since it is well known that constipation has always been associated with melancholy.[60]

It may seem surprising that the subtle, esoteric analyst of seventeenth-century melancholy allegories, with his messianic and metaphysical inclinations, should carry out such a savage anatomy of the melancholy of his contemporaries based on a harsh revolutionary and materialist attitude. It is true that this oscillation was characteristic of Benjamin's personality, and that it constitutes one of the mysteries of his thinking. As well as an outburst of revolutionary militancy it appears to me there is also indignation at his adored melancholy meeting such a mediocre fate by falling into the hands of the despairing pessimism of writers such as Kästner. It should be remembered that scarcely two years later, in 1933, Benjamin recognized his own saturnine melancholy in the text 'Agesilaus Santander'.

Benjamin's anti-melancholy rant should also be seen in the context of the cultural and political battles typical of the Weimar Republic. Against the optimism and hopes that were the driving force behind Expressionism, there arose a current of 'New Objectivity' (*Neue Sachlichkeit*), which Kästner was part of and which was characterized by a disillusioned mixture of resignation and cynicism.[61] Walter Benjamin reacted furiously against this current. In another article from the same period, Benjamin praises Siegfried Kracauer, a writer opposed to New Objectivity, and sees in him a model to follow. Despite his Marxist-Leninist vehemence, he also finds room to express his own peculiar (and unorthodox) vision of the tasks of the left-wing intellectual, who according to him should be seen as a rag-picker. Since it is impossible for the bourgeois intellectual to become part of the proletariat, it is better for him to dedicate himself to politicizing his own class. This intellectual, a son of the bourgeoisie, thus becomes a discontented spoilsport who is both solitary and on the margins. Benjamin describes him as:

A rag-picker in the grey early morning, poking with his stick at the ragged ends of speeches and scraps of language, then tossing them, grumbling, stubborn, a trifle intoxicated, into his barrow, not without letting one or another of these bits of faded cotton, such as 'humanity', 'inwardness' or 'depth' flutter in the morning wind. A rag-picker, early – in the grey dawn of the day of revolution.[62]

How much melancholy there is in these words! The day of revolution never arrived. But fascism did: the rag-picker had to flee and become a *flâneur*.

IN MARCH 1933, pressured by friends who warned him of the imminent dangers threatening him, Benjamin abandoned Germany to begin a reluctant exile. Weary of existence, following two flirtations with suicide, he went to Paris, where he stayed in fleapit hotels and worked hard on his *Arcades Project*. Political contingencies led him to live the life of a wanderer and rag-picker, so that he came to be the living embodiment of the Baudelairian metaphors of the *flâneur* and the *chiffonnier*. Could Benjamin have glimpsed, in his wanderings around Paris, the woman who passed rapidly by him in the street, with her majestic sorrow and deep mourning as Baudelaire describes her in his poem 'À une passante'? Perhaps he felt like the drunken rag-picker whose heart is full of projects, in the Baudelaire poem he so much admired:

> A rag-picker comes into view, nodding his head
> Stumbling and banging into walls like a poet.[63]

In those difficult moments Benjamin could possibly have wished that his subjectivity, which was plunging into the depths of the abyss, might be rescued by the allegorical 'mysterious contemplation' which halts the fall of the Baroque angel in the final paragraphs of his essay on German tragic drama? In his book on Benjamin's melancholy dialectics, Max Pensky mistakenly attributes this concept to Calderón de la Barca.[64] Although Benjamin does not spell it out, it is in fact a quotation from Baltasar Gracián, who devotes two of the discourses in his *Agudeza y arte de ingenio* to it.[65] I wonder if Benjamin ever directly read in Gracián his reflections on mysterious contemplation? I suppose he never did. If he had done so, he would have discovered a fascinating explanation: mysterious contemplation is the subtle method of placing a mystery between two extremes, contingencies or circumstances, in order to contemplate it and then offer a reasoned explanation. One of the examples he gives is of the delightful story, recounted by Clement of Alexandria, about two musicians – Eunomos and Ariston – who are taking part in a contest at Delphi. While Eunomos is playing, one of the strings of his instrument snaps; at that moment a cicada flies by, settles on the peg of the broken string and starts to sing exactly as the missing sounds would have been. How is one to explain the mystery of this 'rare contingency'? According to Gracián, Clement resolves it when he understands that 'the music sounds so pleasant even to Heaven itself that with special providence it favours and authorizes it.'[66] Gracián explains that contingencies are the everyday stuff of mysteries since they give rise to a meditation, a contemplation: 'The more extravagant the contingency, the greater the contemplation . . . The source of these mysterious contemplations is the variety and plurality of circumstances.'[67]

In the scholastic tradition, contingency allows one to demonstrate that events and beings – which could just as easily happen in another way or not occur at all – owe their existence to the Creator. But in Benjamin's day, contingency implies a profound existential angst. The fortuitous event that the cicada took the place of the broken string revealed the presence of a miracle: but in nineteenth-century modernity, it indicates that a break in the string of life can be repaired (or not) thanks to the coincidental flight of a cicada (or butterfly) that succeeds in re-establishing harmony.

It could also be thought that the beauty of the music might have died at the moment when the string snapped, if a cicada had not rescued it from disaster. However that may be, a contingency without a miracle brings us face to face with the absurd.

During the same period in which Benjamin was writing about the Paris of Baudelaire, another philosopher, Jean-Paul Sartre, was working on a book that links contingency to melancholy. This was a topic that was deeply rooted in Existentialist traditions – Kierkegaard, Husserl – as well as in the European crisis following the First World War. Even though Benjamin and Sartre were never in contact, it seems to me that the latter's book on contingency can help us understand the former's predicament. The work was originally called *Factum sur la Contingence*, then *Melancholia* and finally, when it was published in 1937, *La Nausée*.[68] The novel's protagonist, Antoine Roquentin, could almost be a portrait of Walter Benjamin hard at work in the Bibliothèque Nationale in Paris. At a certain moment in the narrative, Roquentin is overwhelmed by a sense of melancholy (nausea) – when he discovers contingency in a bland, insipid world in which mankind is superfluous, unnecessary. But this melancholic nausea allows him to discover freedom in the midst of contingency: a freedom he does not know what to do with.[69] In spite of the pessimism in which the idea of existential nausea is steeped, Sartre's melancholy is the driving force behind a mordant criticism of the stupidity of the modern world in extreme experiences where it is hard to distinguish madness from lucidity. Of course, as Sartre wrote in a preparatory notebook, melancholy nausea is closely linked to the ennui of individuals who live in an alien world surrounded by frustrated, ephemeral little people. In it he asks himself: 'what then is ennui? It's where there is *too much*, and at the same time *there isn't enough*. Not enough because there is too much, too much because there is not enough.'[70]

This digression on Sartre connects us once again with Baudelaire's spleen: the ennui of those people who are sick of memories and lacking curiosity – like the hateful moonlit cemeteries of his verse; immortal beings who lack life are rich but impotent.[71] Without a doubt, with regard to Baudelaire's melancholy, Benjamin has a similar position to the one he adopted towards the Baroque playwrights:

> Baudelaire's genius, which is nourished on melancholy, is an allegorical genius. For the first time, with Baudelaire, Paris becomes the subject of lyric poetry. This poetry is no hymn to the homeland; rather, the gaze of the allegorist as it falls on the city, is the gaze of the alienated man. It is the gaze of the flâneur, whose way of life still conceals behind a mitigating nimbus the coming desolation of the big-city dweller.[72]

Benjamin is once again confronting the problem of the relationship between melancholy and modernity. But now it is no longer a question of the first Baroque light of the modern, but the spectacular forms it acquires in the great urban expansion of the nineteenth century, whose emblematic epicentre is the city of Paris. There he discovers allegorical figures who represent modernity: the bohemian, the rag-picker, the adventurer, the conspirator, the flâneur, the dandy and the hero. In his treatment of the problem, Benjamin reflects on the link between these allegories and the idea of 'nouveauté': 'Just as in the seventeenth century it is allegory that becomes the canon of dialectical images, in the nineteenth century it is novelty.'[73] Thus, modern culture lauds novelties in the market of spiritual values. In addition to their use value, goods acquire an aura that is produced by the 'false consciousness' embodied in fashion.

When Benjamin developed these ideas in another text ('The Paris of the Second Empire in Baudelaire'), he greatly disappointed his friend Theodor Adorno, who had very much liked the idea of 'novelty' as he was convinced that the true mediation between psychology and society is to be found in the fetishization of goods.[74] Adorno points out that Benjamin's analysis establishes a direct, instantaneous link between Baudelaire's metaphors and the economic conditions of the nineteenth century: the *flâneur* circulates in the same way as goods, the images of drunkenness arise from taxes on wine, rag-pickers emerge when the new industrial processes give waste a value, and Parisian fantasies are fuelled by the mercantilism of the writers of serial novels. Benjamin introduces a crude materialism thanks to which he attempts to explain spleen through the mercantile economy. Adorno is surely right when he tells him that his 'study of Goethe's Elective Affinities and the book on the Baroque are better Marxism than your wine tax and your deduction of phantasmagoria from the practices of the feuilletonists developed in 'The Paris of the Second Empire in Baudelaire'.[75]

However, the collection of fragments and quotations gathered in the *Arcades Project* shows that Benjamin was searching for a more profound explanation of the relationship between industrial modernity and melancholy. He stresses the importance of the new and novelty: even the *flâneur* is thirsty for novelties, and slakes that thirst in the crowd.[76] It is typical of advanced capitalism that in order to stimulate demand it promotes novel products, while at the same time the 'eternal return of the same' is shown by the mass production of goods.[77] This dialectic determines the contradictory links between the cult of the new and the ennui produced by the endless repetition of the same. This alienating process produces the agony of a new kind of spleen, a feeling of living permanently in a catastrophe.[78] I sense in this a kind of negative Hegelianism. Whereas Hegel was enthusiastic about the arrival of a new age, Benjamin saw this as a misfortune. But in both of them, ennui seems to be the herald of novelty. In the prologue to his *Phenomenology of Spirit* of 1807, Hegel writes:

Frivolity and ennui, which are spreading in the established order of things, the undefined foreboding of something unknown – all these betoken that there is something else approaching. This gradual crumbling to pieces, which did not alter the general look and aspect of the whole, is interrupted by the sunrise, which, in a flash and a single stroke, brings to view the form and structure of the new world.[79]

For Benjamin, the new means the arrival of the horrendous capitalist industrial modernity, which brings ennui and spleen trailing in its wake. In some of his writing, he appears to admit that the allegorical power of melancholy acts as a stimulus to Baudelaire's genius, and creates the critical possibility of redemption. The genius of melancholy and spirituality are powers that find expression in the effects of hashish and stimulate allegorical imagination.[80] It was impossible not to realize that Baudelaire's melancholy is what converts his extraordinary vision of modernity into poetry and a mordant critique of industrial society. It is melancholy which reveals itself, in all its monstrous decadence, in ennui. The spleen of capitalism distorts the old allegorist who assigned *meanings* to things, turning him into a character who now assigns them a *value* as goods.[81]

In spite of all Benjamin's efforts, his attempts at getting to the bottom of the links between nineteenth-century modernity and melancholy end in failure. Even though he often has intuitions and insights, he does not succeed in making definitive progress towards interpreting Baudelaire's concept of spleen, or more widely in his understanding of the relations between poetry and capitalism. As Adorno remarked, one of his limitations comes from his rash use of a poorly digested Marxism and a materialism that owes more to his noble sentiments than to any thought-through knowledge. The hundreds of fragments collected in the *Arcades Project* give the impression that, lost in the thick forest, Benjamin was going round in circles rather than advancing. The results are the ruined fragments of a labyrinth which have been held up as the best example of Benjamin's method of approaching modernity. That may be so. But it is also true that they are the traces of the Berlin philosopher's angst in his fruitless search for redemption.

ONE OF BENJAMIN's most famous allegories concerns a strange automatic redemption machine that can always defeat any opponent at chess. It is to be found in the first thesis of his last book, *On the Concept of History*, written early in 1940, shortly before he died. This is the legend of an automaton disguised as a Turk that plays chess on a table that conceals, through a system of mirrors, a tiny human being: a hunchback dwarf who is a chess grandmaster and who uses strings to control the mechanical hand moving the pieces. In the philosophical counterpart, Benjamin explains, the puppet is called 'historical materialism' and always wins: 'It can easily be a match for anyone if it enlists the services of theology, which today, as we know, is small and ugly and has to keep out of sight.'[82] Many years before, in 1810, Kleist had told another story. In it, the human being is a famous dancer who visits a puppet theatre, where to his astonishment he discovers that the dancing puppet is infinitely more elegant than him. Since the puppet moves unconsciously, it possesses a perfect grace because it is in harmony with its surroundings, whereas the dancer is self-conscious and as a result isolates himself, becomes distant and mannered. Kleist sees human beings' self-consciousness as a poor imitation of the divinity's all-seeing awareness, to which possibly poets and abandoned lovers can come near. Following on from Kleist, Rilke introduces an angel onto the stage at the puppet theatre. In *The Duino Elegies* he also prefers the puppets, which are complete and in harmony with themselves, to the disguised dancer with a half-finished mask. In the theatre of life the real performance only begins once the angel appears, helps the puppets get to their feet and 'then what we separate merely by being comes together.'[83]

For his part, the hunchback theologian invoked by Benjamin also brings the angel of history to his aid, as well as pulling the strings of the Marxist puppet, which in this allegorical theatre has only a superficial elegance and grace. Benjamin's vision is as tragic and bitter as Kleist or Rilke's: mankind's redemption depends on a mechanical puppet manipulated by a metaphysical dwarf and, possibly, by an angel who looks on in astonishment at how the wreckage left by the storm of history piles up in front of his eyes.

In German literature there is another symptomatic example of the link between angels and automatons. In a satirical piece written in 1785 by Jean-Paul entitled *Men Are the Machines of Angels*, man appears as an automaton in a materialist and mechanized world. Humanity here needs supernatural beings to act as its guide. The origin of this situation, Jean-Paul writes, goes back to a time when the angels came to our world, as yet uninhabited. Little by little, they invented human automata 'until progressively their most brilliant machines, or men, were sufficient for their needs'. Jean-Paul's mechanical men are lifeless creatures without identity, mere pawns the angels play chess with or vulgar praying machines, according to Alain Montandon.[84] These angels are beings who perform and reveal hidden meanings.

By contrast, Rilke's angels are similar to those of Islam, as he himself explained; they are beings in which the transformation of the visible into the invisible takes place: for the angel of the *Duino Elegies* all the towers and palaces of other epochs exist clearly, whilst those in our present existence have already become invisible: 'he is a being charged with recognizing in the invisible a higher level of reality.'[85] In Benjamin's case, the angel of history invoked in the ninth thesis of 1940 can only see the past, as he turns his back on the future:

Where we perceive a chain of events, he sees one single catastrophe that keeps piling wreckage on wreckage and hurls it in front of his feet. The angel would like to stay, awaken the dead, and make whole what has been smashed. But a storm is blowing from Paradise; it has got caught in his wings with such violence that the angel can no longer close them. This storm irresistibly propels him into the future to which his back is turned, while the pile of debris before him grows skyward. This storm is what we call progress.[86]

What does this allegory mean? I am inclined to accept Gershom Scholem's suggestion: this is the angel of melancholy.[87] Benjamin's description links it to Klee's *Angelus Novus*, but in fact the images by Dürer, Cranach or Valdés Leal could better illustrate the angel of history. I have already mentioned that the history of melancholy, unlike its psychoanalytic interpretation, demonstrates that the sad task of mourning strengthens that creative or visionary subject. Paradoxically, the very loss of the erotic object becomes an artistic or intellectual object. The creator's suffering is turned into an object of contemplation and admiration. The melancholy angel of history has lost its beloved beings, and the past lies in ruins. Like the allegorist, the angel offers us a new meaning: there is no great chain of events; in its place there is a huge catastrophe. The angel in Dürer's engraving has a vision that creative melancholy has produced. In losing the original object of his desire, the angel of melancholy finds it again in his visionary trance. However, the viewer cannot look at what Dürer's angel (or the Angelus Novus) can see. However, he can decipher or intuit it. All that remain are signs and emblems which can reveal the key to us. Of course, the most visible icon is the angel himself. But neither the object nor the subject is visible. In losing the beloved object, the angel constructs it as a melancholy vision. The angel himself is not the subject: he is there to represent it symbolically. Thus, in Dürer, Benjamin and many others, thanks to the deployment of sophisticated, complex theological and allegorical resources, the loss of the desired object generates a melancholy force that is able to weave an emotional and conceptual fabric that for centuries has been a fundamental underpinning of modern culture.

Walter Benjamin lends great importance to the dialectical image in our knowledge of the historical past; that is what presents itself to the angel:

> The true image of the past *flits by*. The past can only be seized as an image that flashes up at the moment of its recogniz-ability, and is never seen again.[88]

This fleeting image reminds me of those still-lifes of allegorical objects known as *vanitas*, originally created by Flemish painters. A collection of objects such as skulls, flowers, clocks, crystal jugs, globes, crowns, sceptres, jewels, playing cards, wax candles, books and many other things made up the impressive *vanidades* painted by Antonio Pereda and Juan de Valdés Leal in the 1600s, who were able to express the 'disappointments' so characteristic of the conceptual pessimism of Gracián or Quevedo during the Spanish '*Siglo de Oro*'. Their painted hieroglyphs symbolized the fleeting nature of existence, the sterility of power and worldly glories, the passage of time that turns everything into ruins and dust, the fragility of life, the ephemeral nature of knowledge and the disillusions of pleasures.[89]

In his fleeting images, Benjamin seeks to rescue the history of the defeated from the continuity of the history of the victors. As in *vanitas* paintings, the melancholy vision dissolves the conformist power of the victors in the acid of pointless vanity, and extols the hope of the redemption of the oppressed. The *vanitas* proposed a distancing from the temptations of the world: in a similar vein, Benjamin explains that his theses are born of a resolution similar to the rule in monasteries that, in order to stimulate meditation, taught monks to scorn the world and its ostentation. It is a warning about the dangers of allowing oneself to be taken in by those politicians who, due to their stubborn belief in progress, have failed to stand up against fascism.[90] That is why he criticizes the historicism that seeks empathy in the victors' world of the past and its coveted plunder, the so-called cultural heritage. Benjamin argues that the materialist historian must distance himself from this worldly abundance – full of barbarity and the fruits of exploitation – and be prepared instead for the lightning flash that opens the door to the redeeming Messiah. To get rid of the victors' barbarity, which every cultural document contains, Benjamin says one has to 'rub history against the grain'.[91]

Benjamin's affirmation that historians show an empathy with the victors raises a difficult problem of interpretation, especially if we place it within the context of the obvious sadness that permeates the 1940 theses. In the seventh thesis, Benjamin affirms the origin of this empathy:

> Its origin is indolence of the heart, that *acedia* which despairs of appropriating the genuine historical image as it briefly flashes up. Among medieval theologians acedia was regarded as the root cause of sadness. Flaubert, who was familiar with it, wrote: '*Peu de gens devineront combien il a fallu être triste por ressuciter Carthage*'. The nature of this sadness becomes clearer if we ask: With whom does historicism actually sympathise? The answer is inevitable: with the victor.[92]

An explanation typical of optimistic Marxism tells us that acedia is the feeling of melancholy in the face of fatality that robs all the actions of human beings of any value. The epitome of a melancholy person, dominated by acedia, would therefore be the courtier, who is by nature a traitor, since his surrender to fate leads him always to side with the victor.[93] This is a partial interpretation that arises from what Benjamin himself says about acedia in his essay on German tragic drama. It is true that Benjamin says that acedia was 'the genuinely theological conception of the melancholic'.[94] It is also true that during the Middle Ages and Renaissance, a link was established between acedia and melancholy, two sicknesses that shared many symptoms and appeared with very similar images. However, both theologians and doctors were well aware that the former was a *mortal sin*, whereas the latter was a physical illness that produced a mental disorder. As a sin, acedia was the result of a free choice by the person who allowed himself to be possessed by ennui towards life and sloth. As an illness, melancholy was produced by the internal conflagration of the bodily humours, independently of the will of the person affected.[95] Benjamin, despite being to some extent aware of these differences, finds that the melancholy of the tyrant or courtier is more revealing when considered as acedia. He is mistaken, and his analysis is inaccurate, because the traits that he sees in 'saturnine acedia' (apathy, infidelity, indecision, sloth, despair, sadness) are all equally symptoms of those suffering from melancholy. What is strange about acedia is its moral dimension, which is absent in those affected by the black, harsh humours. Moreover, it should be pointed out that Benjamin's essay on Baroque drama is full of subtleties. Considering acedia as betrayal and infidelity, at the end of his comments Benjamin refers to its 'dialectic contrary', in a beautiful and impressive formulation: 'Melancholy betrays the world for the sake of knowledge. But in its tenacious self-absorption it embraces dead objects in its contemplation, in order to redeem them.'[96] Is this not exactly what the melancholy angel of history proposes? The problem is that when Benjamin refers to acedia in his theses on the concept of history, he is using the term in its ancient theological-moral sense, as it was applied in monasteries in the time of Casiano (John Cassian). It is not in fact a reference to melancholy.

The angel of history is able to recognize in the past the ruins of a great catastrophe: not because it suffers from sinful acedia and sadness, but because it possesses the allegorical and contemplative power that melancholy conveys. In this context, what is the meaning of the allegory of the Turkish automaton that wins every chess game? I do not know whether Benjamin knew of Jean-Paul's text on the angels and their machines. It is likely that he was aware of Rilke's angels, and we know for certain he had read Kleist's essay, since he quotes from it in an article entitled 'In Praise of Marionettes', published in 1930. In it he refers to the memorable image of how Kleist's marionette 'confronts God, with destitute man dangling between the two of them in his thoughtful enclosure'.[97] Among the triad of allegorical beings, only one of them, the human being (the tiny hunchback) is capable of acting on his own. The angel is paralysed, and the Turkish puppet lacks a life of its own. While it is true that the angel of history is able to offer a correct melancholy vision of the past, and the mechanical puppet confronts his adversary, only theology, shut in its hiding place, can pull the strings of historical materialism. Benjamin does not appear to have any special taste or enthusiasm for the movements of the chess-playing puppet, which seems more like Jean-Paul's absurd praying machine, invented to serve the angels. The idea that the puppet is secretly manipulated by a dwarf comes from Edgar Allan Poe, who was present at several performances of the chess-playing automaton put on by the musician and engineer Johann Nepomuk Maelzel in the United States. This marvellous contraption had originally been presented at the court of Vienna by Baron Wolfgang von Kempelen in 1769; it was later acquired by Maelzel, the inventor of a mechanical orchestra, the Panharmonicon, for which Beethoven composed his *Battle of Vitoria Symphony* (1813). Edgar Allan Poe provided a rational explanation of the automaton's mysterious workings: he imagined that Maelzel's assistant, a misshapen dwarf, was hidden inside the apparatus.[98] Benjamin took this idea, but restored its irrational, enigmatic flavour: historical materialism always wins the game thanks to theology. In other words, rationalism cannot function without metaphysics, and the Marxist historians inherit a kind of weak messianic force to which the past lays claim.[99]

It is not easy, from a rationalist perspective, to accept Benjamin's theological proposal. Why would modern historical science need the aid of metaphysical dwarves and melancholy angels? There has been much debate and a good few interpretations of this. I personally like an idea of Adorno's that suggests a reply: 'did not recognize in any of its manifestations the obvious limit of all modern thought: Kant's injunction not to take flight towards unintelligible worlds.'[100] We should understand from this that Benjamin turned to theology, as well as melancholy meditation, so as not to drown when swimming in the deep waters of the seas of chaos. Rationalism and historical materialism were not enough to guide him on his perilous journey through the abysses: he needed the dwarf and the angel.

BENJAMIN NAVIGATED HIS tempestuous times as though he were travelling through an unintelligible world. He contemplated modernity around him as if it were in ruins, and picked up fragments to classify in his collection of allegorical images. From the start of his exile in 1933, he kept the hope that, at a moment when he was least expecting it, a dialectical image would flash for a few seconds, open a window onto the nineteenth century for him, and allow him to glimpse the secrets of modernity. He did not like the world he was passing through, which he saw as being dominated by a threatening capitalism; he believed that the magical flame had not gone out which with its dim light still allowed one to see an enchanted panorama where, to use his own words: 'the observer is confronted with the *facies hippocratica* of history as a petrified, primordial landscape.'[101] Weber had postulated that capitalism encouraged the extinction of magic and myth. Benjamin on the other hand understood that modern society was still under the spell of mythological dreams, as he pointed out in the *Arcades Project*: 'Capitalism was a natural phenomenon with which a new dream-filled sleep came over Europe, and, through it, a reactivation of mythic forces.'[102] However, he did not see in this a romantic rebirth of Novalis's beautiful blue flower, but rather the sick face of encroaching death. In a short essay written at the time he was studying German tragic drama, he observed that Surrealism was proposing a new way of dreaming:

> No longer does the dream reveal a blue horizon. The dream has grown grey. The grey coating of dust on things is its best part. Dreams are now a shortcut to banality.[103]

This implies that even the Surrealist dream imagination is linked to the kitsch of mass culture. It might also be said that, in Benjamin's view, modernity converted the brilliant black sun of melancholy into the dull grey star of ennui. Somehow, the dark, melancholy and solitary bird of night, illuminated by the lamp of genius, which according to Diderot split the silence and shadows with its melodious song,[104] has turned into the black crow that, in Edgar Allan Poe's great poem, repeats the same word over and over: Nevermore . . . Never again will the bird's sharp beak be torn from the heart, never again will the soul be able to free itself from the shadow of this bird of ill-omen.

It could be said that Benjamin was driven by melancholy but succumbed to ennui. We know that ennui, spleen, acedia, weariness and boredom are the different facets of the crystal of melancholy. But they are not exactly the same. Benjamin was interested in a book by Emile Tardieu, *L'Ennui* (1903), which he saw as a kind of humorous compendium of the twentieth century. Tardieu saw all human activity as a vain attempt to escape boredom. In him, Benjamin finds another example of the sterile petit-bourgeois discontent that reduces all heroism and asceticism to ennui.[105] In 1926, the same book caught the attention of the brilliant psychologist Pierre Janet, who was doubtful about the interpretation of ennui as arising from depression. His clinical practice indicated that in states of deep melancholy the sufferers showed no sign of ennui or boredom; it was only in cases of slight depression that boredom was a factor. Janet points out that ennui is not linked to the paralysing inactivity that afflicts melancholics; he notes that in literature, apathetic authors such as Amiel make no mention of boredom, whereas hyperactive writers such as Chateaubriand and Flaubert speak all the time of their profound boredom.[106] Thus what takes place in asylums and with psychiatrists' patients is not the same as that which we can observe in cultural spaces. Ennui and melancholy are not bedfellows in the Salpêtrière hospital, but they meet in *Les Fleurs du mal*. Referring to Baudelaire's poems, Benjamin said that 'The awareness of time's empty passage and the *tædium vitæ* are the two weights that keep the wheels of melancholy going.'[107] He was referring to the poem 'L'Horloge' and to the sequence on death in *Les Fleurs du mal*.

Did Benjamin feel the weight of boredom during the long hours he spent studying in the Bibliothèque Nationale in Paris; in Ibiza where he suffered hardships and rebuffs; in the concentration camp near Nevers where he was interned? However that may be, it is quite likely that he felt that the passage of time, filled as it was with the threat of war, produced a kind of void around him, and yet he rejected the role of the fortune-teller who, by looking into the future, avoids experiencing time as empty and homogeneous. He preferred the ancient Jewish tradition that prohibited any scanning of the future but instead praised the recollection of times gone by. 'This disenchanted the future,' he wrote, 'which holds sway over all those who turn to soothsayers for enlightenment. This does not imply, however, that for the Jews the future became homogeneous, empty time, for every second was the small gateway through which the Messiah might appear.'[108]

Knowing the future that awaited him in Portbou, we may surmise that, when the narrow door opened for him and he saw that the Redeemer did not appear, Walter Benjamin took advantage of that fleeting instant to escape before the door closed once more.

In May 1940, when Hitler's armies began their march on Paris, together with millions of others Benjamin fled towards the south of France. He left the manuscript of the *Arcades Project* with his friend Georges Bataille, who hid it in the Bibliothèque Nationale. He spent part of that summer in Lourdes, waiting for an entry permit to the United States. At the end of August, he travelled to Marseilles, where Horkheimer had succeeded in getting him a visa at the U.S. consulate. However, Benjamin did not have all the necessary documents, and so he decided to cross into Spain illegally, and from there make his way to Portugal and then embark for America. At dawn on 26 September he set out from Banyuls-sur-Mer to walk across the mountains and enter Spain clandestinely. The small group he crossed the Pyrenees with reached Portbou that afternoon. There the Francoist police informed them that their transit visas had just been cancelled on government orders, and that they had to return to France the following day. That night, in the hotel where they were staying, Benjamin took a strong dose of morphine and crossed through the narrow door to death. Many of the commentaries and reflections on Benjamin's life give the sense that this tragic end was pre-ordained in his character or destiny. Everything in his life seemed to conspire to lead him towards suicide. And yet, as far as we know, it was contingency – what has been called a stroke of bad luck – that decided Benjamin's fate in Portbou. As Hannah Arendt observes:

> One day earlier, Benjamin would have got through without any trouble; one day later the people in Marseilles would have known that for the time being it was impossible to

pass through Spain. Only on that particular day was the catastrophe possible.[109]

A day after Benjamin's death, an unexpected storm persuaded the Spanish police not to send Benjamin's companions back, and in the end they were authorized to continue on their way to Portugal (with the help of a large bribe).[110] If that storm, which I would like to think was a delayed reaction to the blink of the Frankfurt professors, had arrived a little earlier, Walter Benjamin would not have left Marseilles or taken his own life in Portbou. However, many will say he was bound to have committed suicide at some point, at a moment when bad luck made him panic, because, as Arendt believed, Benjamin had an infallible gift for being in the wrong place at the wrong time.

Benjamin's death is often seen as an enigma, a mystery. Not only have the exact circumstances remained obscure, but the tragic final sequence of events seems like an invitation to search for a hidden logic in his life, his work and his circumstances. In other words, in his depressive character, his texts full of melancholy signs, and an overpowering fascism that liquidated people like Benjamin. It is true that the pieces of the jigsaw puzzle fit perfectly, and the image that appears is very logical, all too logical: that of the enigmatic, sad Jewish intellectual who was a victim of Nazism. I suspect that Benjamin would not have been pleased with this mythical image of his death. He would possibly have preferred to be remembered as a revolutionary who had lived in constant danger, who had risked raising a bucket full of melancholy from the abysmal well of the Baroque past. Who had dared to drink down the humour he had found there to fortify himself, and who later had gone to look in Baudelaire's Paris for the keys to modern ennui. Who had understood he had to search for that dangerous moment when the past reveals itself. Who when he found it, had yanked on the emergency brake to stop the frantic train of progress. And who at that very moment had leapt towards the past like a tiger through a carriage door. Who had caused the train to derail. Who had achieved an implosion of the past. Who at the moment of the interruption of the future had glimpsed the whole of history as summarized and crystallized in the here-and-now of Portbou. Who, surrounded by danger, had been unable either to advance or retreat. Who neither the angel of melancholy nor the hunchback theologian had been able to save. Who had hoped for redemption at that moment, but who had preferred to put out the light rather than be disappointed. Who had understood that darkness would save him.

References

Prologue

1 Claude Lévi-Strauss, *Tristes Tropiques* (Paris, 1955), pp. 376ff.
2 Friedrich von Schiller, 'On the Sublime', in *Two Essays*, trans. Julius A. Elias (New York, 1966), p. 204.
3 Apocalypse 21:17. Paul Claudel brought together his reflections on angels, initiated in Frankfurt in 1910, in 'Notes sur les anges', part of his book *Présence et prophétie* (*Œuvres complètes*, xx, pp. 370–431; the quote comes from a 1941 letter, on p. 427).

ONE

**Melancholy as a Critique of Reason:
Kant and Sublime Madness**

1 'Die Schwermutsschnellen hindurch/ am blanken/ Wundenspiegel vorbei/ da warden die vierzig/ entrindeten Lebensbäume geflösst.' 'Atemkristall', translated from German by Pierre Joris: https://doubleoperative.files.wordpress.com/2009/12/celans-breathcrystal.doc.
2 Reinhold Bernhard Jachmann, *Emmanuel Kant raconté dans des lettres à un ami*, trans. Jean Mostler, in *Kant intime* (Paris, 1985), p. 43.
3 Manfred Kuehn, *Kant: A Biography* (Cambridge, 2001), p. 66.
4 Reinhardt Brandt, 'Kant en Königsberg', in *Immanuel Kant: política, derecho y antropología* (Mexico, 2001), p. 51.
5 Ludwig Ernest Borowski, *Relato de la vida y el carácter de Immanuel Kant* [*Darstellung des Lebens und des Charakters Immanuel Kants*, Königsberg, 1804] (Madrid, 1993), p. 129.

6   The translation is from Immanuel Kant, *Observations on the Feeling of the Beautiful and Sublime and Other Writings*, ed. Patrick Frierson and Paul Guyer (Cambridge, 2011), p. 205.

7   Immanuel Kant, 'Essay on the Maladies of the Head', in *The Cambridge Edition of the Works of Immanuel Kant: Anthropology, History and Education* (Cambridge, 2011), p. 214.

8   *Bemerkungen zu den Beobachtungen überdas Gefühl des Schönen und Erhabenen* (Note to *Observations on the Feeling of the Beautiful and Sublime*), quoted by Arsenij Gulyga, *Immanuel Kant: His Life and Thought* (Boston, MA, 1987), p. 43.

9   Kant, *Observations on the Feeling of the Beautiful and Sublime and Other Writings*, p. 205.

10 See Isaiah Berlin: *The Magus of the North: J. G. Hamann and the Origins of Modern Irrationalism*, ed. Henry Hardy (London, 1993).

11 Kant, *Observations on the Feeling of the Beautiful and Sublime and Other Writings*, p. 206.

12 Ibid., p. 212.

13 Ibid.

14 Immanuel Kant, *Antropología práctica (según el manuscrito inédito de C. C. Mrongovius, 1785)*, trans. Roberto Rodríguez Aramayo (Madrid, 1990), p. 12. Kant published his description of the four temperaments in his *Anthropology* of 1798 (see 'Anthropology from a Practical Point of View', in *The Cambridge Edition of the Works of Immanuel Kant: Anthropology, History and Education*, ed. Günter Zöller and Robert B. Louden (Cambridge, 2007). He frequently uses the notion of enthusiast and enthusiasm, as was common from the seventeenth century onwards, to refer to individuals with supposed prophetic capabilities and to puritan, millenarist, anabaptist or other sects. See, for example, the book by Henry More, the great Cambridge neo-platonist philosopher, *Enthusiasmus Triumphatus, or, A Discourse of the Nature, Causes, Kinds, and Cure of Enthusiasme* (London, 1662). In his book, More refers to melancholy, epilepsy and hysteria to explain the natural causes of enthusiasm (pp. 1–15).

15 Kant, *Observations on the Feeling of the Beautiful and Sublime and Other Writings*, p. 214.

16 Ibid., p. 217.

17 Manfred Kuehn, in his extensive biography of Kant, strangely
    downplays this work, which he sees merely as a reflection of the
    prejudices of the time (*Kant: A Biography*, p. 142). Kuehn fails to
    explore the theme of melancholy and its relation to the idea of
    the sublime, and in so doing sidelines a significant part of Kant's
    life and thought. He only considers the superficial pathological
    aspects of hypochondria (pp. 151–2). Nor does he take into account
    the essay on the maladies of the head. Nor does Susan Meld Shell,
    in a very interesting chapter devoted to Kant's hypochondria in
    her book, *The Embodiment of Reason: Kant on Spirit, Generation,
    and Community* (Chicago, IL, 1996), pay much attention to
    his book on the beautiful and sublime. This is because, despite
    stressing the importance of Kant's ideas on hypochondria among
    his philosophical achievements, Shell reduces hypochondria to
    its pathological or somatic dimensions, and does not explore its
    connections with the sublime or with melancholy.
18 *A Philosophical Enquiry into the Origin of Our Ideas of the Sublime
    and Beautiful*, ed. James T. Boulton (Oxford, 1987), I: vii: 29.
19 Ibid., IV: vi: 221.
20 See the commentaries on Haller's *Unvolkommene Ode uber die
    Ewigkeit* in the book by Anselm Haverkamp, *Leaves of Mourning:
    Hölderlin's Late Work* (Albany, NY, 1995), pp. 22ff.
21 Kant, *Observations on the Feeling of the Beautiful and Sublime and
    Other Writings*, p. 26.
22 In 1785 (*Antropología práctica*, p. 16) Kant expresses a very different
    opinion of the phlegmatic, in whom he sees insensitivity and
    apathy only in their weakest sense. The phlegmatic temperament
    in its strong sense is the most favoured temperament, the one
    associated with philosophers and the ability to judge.
23 'Il Penseroso' and 'L'Allegro'; see John Milton, *Il Penseroso and The
    Allegro* (with paintings by William Blake) (New York, 1954).
24 Kant, *Observations on the Feeling of the Beautiful and Sublime*, p. 26n.
25 Ibid., p. 17n.
26 Ernst Cassirer, *Kant's Life and Thought*, trans. James Haden
    (New Haven, CT, 1981), p. 215.
27 Gulyga, *Immanuel Kant: His Life and Thought*, p. 52.
28 Kant, *Dreams of a Spirit-seer Elucidated by Dreams of
    Metaphysics: Cambridge Edition of the Works of Immanuel Kant,*

Theoretical Philosophy, 1755–1770, trans. and ed. David Walford
(Cambridge, 1992), p. 305.

29 Ibid., p. 346.

30 Ibid., p. 347.

31 This letter has only survived in a transcription, without doubt
'arranged', by Ludwig Ernst Borowski, which features as an
appendix to his *Relato de la vida y el character de Immanuel Kant*.

32 *Dreams of a Spirit-seer Elucidated by Dreams of Metaphysics*,
p. 341.

33 Ibid., p. 352.

34 Kant thought that the author was Swift. It has also been attributed
to Pope, and was probably a collective work to which John
Arbuthnot also contributed. Martinus Scriblerus, *Peri Bathos:
Of the Art of Sinking in Poetry, Written in the Year* MDCCXXVII,
in *The Works of Alexander Pope*, ed. Joseph Warton, vol. VI
(London, 1803). In a letter to Herder from April 1783, Hamann
tells him he has visited Kant, who 'is the most careful observer
of his *evacuations*, and often ruminates on them in the most
inappropriate places, examining this matter so indelicately that
one is often tempted to laugh in his face. This almost happened
today, but I assured him that the smallest oral or written evacuation
caused me difficulties as great as the *a posteriori* evacuations he
produced' (quoted by Kuehn, *Kant: A Biography*, p. 239).

35 *Dreams of a Spirit-seer Elucidated by Dreams of Metaphysics*, p. 336.
He is referring to the verses 772–81 of Canto 3 of the second part
of *Hudibras*, as follows: 'As *wind* in th' *Hypocondries* pend/ Is but
a blast if downward sent;/ But if upwards chance to fly/ Becomes
new *Light* and *Prophesy*:/ So when your Speculations tend/ Above
their just and useful end:/ Although they promise strange and
great/ *Discoveries* of things far set/ They are but idle dreams and
fancies/ And savour strongly of the *Ganzas*.' Samuel Butler wrote
almost two hundred prose sketches of different 'characters' in
the manner of Theophrastus. Among them there is one devoted
to the melancholy man, where Butler emphasizes his 'visionary'
side: 'His Sleeps and his Wakings are so much the same that he
knows not how to distinguish them, and many times when he
dreams, he believes he is broad awake and sees visions.' Further
on, he writes: 'He converses with nothing so much as his own

Imagination, which being apt to misrepresent THINGS to him, makes him believe that it is something else than that it is, and that he holds Intelligence with spirits . . . He makes the infinity of his Temper pass for Revelations, as Mahomet did by his falling sickness (Samuel Butler, 'A Melancholy Man', *Characters* (1659). Reproduced in the anthology of texts on melancholy collected by Jennifer Radden, *The Nature of Melancholy* (Oxford, 2000), pp. 158–9. In the poem, *Ganzas* is a reference to the geese that take the protagonist to the Moon in the work by the English bishop Francis Godwin: *The Man in the Moone: or, a Discourse of a Voyage Thither by Domingo Gonsales, the Speedy Messenger* (London, 1638).

36 Hamann indirectly reproached Kant for enclosing himself in a purely rational metaphysics. In 1771 he translated and published, in the *Königsberger gelehrte Zeitung*, the conclusion to the first book of *A Treatise on Human Nature* by David Hume. He used a title that recalled the melancholy lying in wait for those who contemplate the immense, dark depths of philosophical problems. In an allusion to the famous poem by Edward Young, the title of his translation was 'Night Thoughts of a Skeptic'. Hume's text reveals his despair because due to his weak faculties, he is shipwrecked on his journey to grasp the great philosophical problems: 'And the impossibility of amending or correcting these faculties, reduces me almost to despair, and makes me resolve to perish on the barren rock, on which I am at present, rather than venture myself upon that boundless ocean, which runs out into immensity. This sudden view of my danger strikes me with melancholy; and as it is usual for that passion, above all others, to indulge itself; I cannot forbear feeding my despair, with all those desponding reflections, which the present subject furnishes me with in such abundance' (quoted by Kuehn in his *Kant: A Biography*, pp. 198–200).

37 Gulyga, *Immanuel Kant: His Life and Thought*, p. 54.

38 Letter dated 8 April 1766, in Cassirer, *Kant's Life and Thought*, p. 79.

39 Kant, *Dreams of a Spirit-seer Elucidated by Dreams of Metaphysics*, p. 337.

40 Kant, *Critique of the Power of Judgment*, trans. Paul Guyer and Eric Matthews (Cambridge, 2000), p. 149.

41 Ibid., p. 208.

42 Isaiah Berlin, *The Roots of Romanticism* (Princeton, NJ, 1999), p. 68.

43 Milton Scarborough, *Myth and Modernity: Postcritical Reflections* (Albany, NY, 1994), p. 105.

44 Friedrich Creuzer, *Symbolik und Mythologie des alten Völker, besonden der Grieschen*, four vols (Leipzig/Darmstadt, 1810–12), IV: pp. 529–31. Quoted and commented on by Félix Duque in his interesting introduction to the Spanish version of another book by Creuzer: see 'Introducción' to the Spanish trans. of Creuzer's *Sileno. Idea y validez del simbolismo antiguo* (Barcelona, 1991), pp. 25ff.

45 Rudolf Otto, *Le Sacré*, trans. André Jundt (Paris, 1995), pp. 27ff and 165.

46 Ernst Cassirer, *Language and Myth*, trans. Susanne K. Langer (New York, 1953), p. 10.

47 Jachmann, *Emmanuel Kant raconté dans des lettres à un ami*, p. 41.

48 According to the reconstruction of the letter, whose original has been lost, based on a draft in German and a translation into Russian, made by Gulyga, *Immanuel Kant: His Life and Thought*, pp. 265–6. Prince Alexandr Mijailovich Beloselsky (1762–1808) is the author of *Dianyologie ou tableau philosophique de l'entendement*, published (in French) in Dresden in 1790. Kant considered the book 'excellent'.

49 Kant, 'Anthropology from a Practical Point of View', p. 247.

50 Cassirer (*Kant's Life and Thought*, p. 408), says that this *Anthropology* is nothing more than a pragmatic pulling together of the abundant material Kant had gathered in his study of mankind throughout his long life, and only devotes a few lines to it. Gulyga, on the other hand, affirms that this book, the last that Kant himself prepared for publication, is one of his most formally lucid works, and ought to be the starting point for an understanding of the philosopher, as his thought can be better understood when read backwards chronologically (*Immanuel Kant: His Life and Thought*, p. 240).

51 'Anthropology from a Practical Point of View', p. 317.

52 Borowski, *Relato de la vida y el carácter de Immanuel Kant*, p. 76.

53 'Anthropology from a Practical Point of View', p. 318.

54 Quoted by Reinhardt Brandt, 'Kant en Königsberg', in *Immanuel Kant: política, derecho y antropología* (Mexico, 2001), p. 59.

55 'Anthropology from a Practical Point of View', p. 321.

56 Ibid., p. 309.

57 Ibid., p. 316 and *Critique of the Power of Judgment*, p. 180.

58 Jean-François Lyotard, *Leçons sur l'analytique du sublime* (Paris, 1991), Chapter Six.

59 See the final pages of Lyotard's *La Condition postmoderne. Rapport sur le savoir* (Paris, 1979).

60 Kant, *Crítica del juicio*, trans. Alejo García Moreno and Juan Rovira (Madrid, 1876), § 23.

61 The others were: 20 on theoretical physics, 16 on mathematics, 12 on law, 11 on an encyclopedia of the philosophical sciences, 4 on pedagogy, 2 on mechanics, 1 on mineralogy and another on theory (Gulyga, *Immanuel Kant: His Life and Thought*, p. 231).

62 *Critique of the Power of Judgment*, p. 116.

63 Wolf Lepenies, *Melancholy and Society*, trans. J. Gaines and D. Jones (Cambridge, MA, 1992), p. 79.

64 Letter to Hufeland, 15 March 1797, quoted by M. J. van Lieburg, *The Discourse of the Learned* (Rotterdam, 1990), p. 83.

65 Jachmann, *Emmanuel Kant raconté dans des lettres à un ami*, p. 41.

66 It is symptomatic that Baudelaire dedicated a poem in the 'Spleen et ideal' section of *Les Fleurs du mal* to the theme of the famous work by Terence, 'L'héautontimorouménos'.

67 *Der Streit der Facultäten*, in M. J. van Lieburg, *The Disease of the Learned: A Chapter from the History of Melancholy and Hypochondria* (Oss, Netherlands 1990), pp. 82–3. The third part of this book refers to the 'Conflict between the faculty of philosophy and the faculty of medicine', and consists of 'a letter to the court advisor and professor Hufeland'.

68 Ehrgott André Ch. Wasianski, *Emmanuel Kant dans les Dernières Années*, trans. Jean Mostler, in *Kant intime* (Paris, 1985). Thomas de Quincey, in *The Last Days of Kant*, wrote a moving English version of Wasianski's testimony, with added material from Jachmann and Borowksi. Wasianski says that at the foot of Kant's body, which was laid out for several days in his house following his death, a poet had left a poem entitled 'To the Shades of Kant'. Wasianski says that

it was possibly a beautiful poem, but that neither he nor his friends could understand its 'sublime style' (p. 161).

69 Ludwig Ernest Borowski, *Relato de la vida y el carácter de Immanuel Kant*, p. 72.

The Spleen of Capitalism: Weber and the Pagan Ethic

1 'sous la coupole spleenétique du ciel, les pieds plongés dans la poussière d'un sol aussi désolé que ce ciel, ils cheminaient avec la physionomie résignée de ceux qui sont condamnés à espérer toujours.' See Charles Baudelaire, 'Le Spleen de Paris (Petits poèmes en prose)', in *Œuvres complètes* (Paris, 1980), VI, 'Chacun sa chimère'.

2 Marianne Weber, *Max Weber: A Biography*, trans. and ed. Harry Zohn (New York, 1975), pp. 486ff.

3 A full description of this situation can be found in the interesting book by Martin Green, *The von Richthofen Sisters: The Triumphant and the Tragic Modes of Love: Else and Frieda von Richthofen, Otto Gross, Max Weber, and D. H. Lawrence, in the Years 1870–1970* (Albuquerque, NM, 1974). See also the essay by Wolfgang Schwentker, 'Passion as a Mode of Life: Max Weber, the Otto Gross Circle and Eroticism', in *Max Weber and His Contemporaries*, ed. Wolfgang J. Mommsen and Jürgen Osterhammel (London, 1987).

4 Weber, *Max Weber*, p. 487.

5 Max Weber, *The Protestant Ethic and the Spirit of Capitalism*, trans. Talcott Parsons (Los Angeles, CA, 1998), p. 270, n.58. Weber explains this as being due to Pietist influence in Kant's education and the philosopher's Scottish ancestry (origins Kant himself believed in, but which have been proved to be false).

6 This letter is transcribed by Marianne Weber in her *Max Weber: A Biography*, pp. 376–8.

7 Ibid., pp. 177–9.

8 Arthur Mitzman, *The Iron Cage: An Historical Interpretation of Max Weber* (New York, 1970), p. 285. On Weber's sense of guilt, see the same book, Chapter Three, subsections 2 and 4, and Marianne Weber, *Max Weber*, pp. 389–90.

9 Max Weber, *Economy and Society: An Outline of Interpretive Sociology* (Berkeley, CA, 1978), vol. I, p. 589.

10 Weber, *The Protestant Ethic and the Spirit of Capitalism*, p. 57.

11 Daniel Bell, *The Cultural Contradictions of Capitalism* (New York, 1976).

12 Ibid., pp. 21–2.

13 See the study by Martin Green, *Mountain of Truth. The Counterculture Begins: Ascona, 1900–1920* (Hanover, NE, 1986).

14 Weber, *Max Weber: A Biography*, p. 488–9.

15 Otto Gross, *Die cerebrale Sekundärfunction*.

16 Green, *Mountain of Truth*.

17 Max Weber, 'Science as a Vocation', in *From Max Weber: Essays in Sociology*, ed. and trans. H. H. Gerth and C. Wright Mills (Nashville, NE, 1948), p. 156.

18 Weber, *Max Weber*, p. 237.

19 Quoted by Mitzman, *The Iron Cage*, p. 218.

20 Karl Jaspers, preface of 1958 to his 1932 essay: *Max Weber. Politiker, Forscher, Philosoph*. English version: 'Max Weber: Politician, Scientist, Philosopher (1932)', in Karl Jaspers, *On Max Weber* (New York, 1989), p. 34.

21 Peter Gay, *The Bourgeois Experience: Victoria to Freud* (Oxford, 1984), p. 421. La Rochefoucauld's maxim is from *Réflections, sentences et maximes morales*, ed. G. Duplessis (1853), the 1678 edition (p. 60), quoted in Gay, ibid., p. 405.

22 See the evocative sketch that Peter Gay draws of hypocrisy on pp. 404–22 of his book.

23 Kant, 'Anthropology from a Practical Point of View', in *The Cambridge Edition of the Works of Immanuel Kant: Anthropology, History and Education*, ed. Günter Zöller and Robert B. Louden (Cambridge, 2007), p. 428.

24 Quoted by Max Weber in *The Protestant Ethic and the Spirit of Capitalism*, p. 175.

25 Weber, *Max Weber*, pp. 491–2.

26 Ibid., p. 489.

27 *The Protestant Ethic and the Spirit of Capitalism*, p. 105.

28 See the commentaries on this by John Owen King III, *The Iron of Melancholy: Structures of Political Conversion in America from the*

Puritan Conscience to Victorian Neurosis (Middletown, CT, 1983), p. 296.

29 *The Protestant Ethic and the Spirit of Capitalism*, p. 181.

30 Ibid., pp. 108–9.

31 Julius H. Rubin correctly observes that the theme of religious melancholy was not addressed by Weber: Rubin, *Religious Melancholy and Protestant Experience in America* (Oxford, 1994), p. 18.

32 John F. Sena, 'Melancholic Madness and the Puritans', *Harvard Theological Review*, LXVI/3 (1973), pp. 293–309.

33 *An Essay towards the Cure of Religious Melancholy in a Letter to a Gentlewoman Afflicted with It* (London, 1717), pp. 8–9, quoted by Rubin, *Religious Melancholy and Protestant Experience in America*, p. 7.

34 Richard Baxter, *The Saints' Everlasting Rest* (New York, 1850), p. 203.

35 Ibid., pp. 191–2.

36 See the essays by Malcolm H. MacKinnon: 'Part I: Calvinism and the Infallible Assurance of Grace' and 'Part II: Weber's Exploration of Calvinism', *British Journal of Sociology*, 39 (1988), pp. 143–77, 178–210.

37 Malcolm H. MacKinnon, 'The Longevity of the Thesis: A Critique of the Critics', in *Weber's Protestant Ethic: Origins, Evidence, Contexts*, ed. Hartmut Lehmann and Guenther Roth (Cambridge, 1993), p. 217.

38 This was not an original idea of Weber's. In 1886 Frederick Engels, for example, asserted that the Calvinist Reformation 'provided the ideological costume for the second act of the bourgeois revolution, which was taking place in England. Here Calvinism stood the test as the true religious disguise of the interests of the contemporary bourgeoisie' (Engels, 'Ludwig Feuerbach and the End of Classical German Philosophy', in *Karl Marx Frederick Engels Collected Works*, vol. XXVI (New York, 1990), pp. 353–98, p. 386). In 1892 Engels explained the links between bourgeois culture and Calvinism: 'where Luther failed, Calvin won the day. Calvin's creed was one fit for the boldest of the bourgeoisie of his time. His predestination doctrine was the religious expression of the fact that in the commercial world of competition success or failure does not depend upon a man's

activity or cleverness, but upon circumstances uncontrollable by him' (Engels, 'Introduction to *Socialism: Utopian and Scientific*', in *Karl Marx Frederick Engels Collected Works*, vol. xxvii (New York, 1990), pp. 278–302, p. 291).

39 See my book *El Siglo de Oro de la melancolía. Textos españoles y novohispanos sobre las enfermedades del alma* (México, 1998).

40 Weber, *Max Weber*, p. 35.

41 'Zur Lage der bürgerlichen Demokratie in Russland', *Archiv*, 22 (1906), p. 347; see trans. 'Prospects of Democracy in Tsarist Russia', in *Selections in Translation*, ed. W. G. Runciman (Cambridge, 1978), p. 282.

42 *The Protestant Ethic and the Spirit of Capitalism*, p. 91, in the last paragraph of the first part. See the commentaries on this by Klaus Lichtblau, 'The Protestant Ethic versus the "New Ethic"', in *Weber's Protestant Ethic: Origins, Evidence, Contexts*, ed. Hartmut Lehmann and Guenther Roth (Cambridge, 1993), p. 193.

43 Johann Wolfgang Goethe, *Elective Affinities*, trans. R. J. Hollingdale (London, 2005), p. 83.

44 Émile Durkeim, *Le Suicide* (Paris, 1930), pp. 170 and 230.

45 A statistical study carried out in 1966 by an intern in the psychiatric hospitals of Strasbourg (who was also a protestant theologian) concludes that 'the protestant faith contributes a higher proportion of melancholics than the Catholic faith.' Othon Printz, *Mélancolie et confession religieuse. Étude statistique, clinique et psychopathologique*, thesis no. 85 (Strasbourg, 1966), p. 17.

46 Durkeim, *Le Suicide*, p. 31.

47 Ibid., p. 424.

48 Ibid., pp. 229–30.

49 Ibid., p. 230.

50 Ibid., p. 243.

51 Ibid., p. 336.

52 Ibid., pp. 365–6.

53 Ibid., p. 419.

54 Goethe, *Elective Affinities*, p. 217.

55 Letter quoted by Weber, *Max Weber*, p. 155.

56 Weber, 'Science as a Vocation', p. 22.

57 Ibid., pp. 154ff.

58 Ibid., p. 228.

59 John Patrick Diggins, *Max Weber: Politics and the Spirit of Tragedy* (New York, 1996), p. 274.

60 Friedrich von Schiller, 'On the Sublime', in *Two Essays*, trans. Julius A. Elias (New York, 1966), p. 198.

61 Ibid., p. 203.

62 Isaiah Berlin, *The Roots of Romanticism* (Princeton, NJ, 1999), p. 81.

63 Charles Baudelaire, 'L'Idéal', from 'Les Fleurs du mal', XVIII, in *Œuvres complètes* (Paris, 1980).

64 Weber, 'Science as a Vocation', p. 218.

65 Ibid., pp. 229–30.

66 'Cette vie est un hôpital où chaque malade est possédé du désir de changer de lit.' Baudelaire, 'Anywhere out of the World', from 'Le Spleen de Paris (Petits poèmes en prose)', XLVIII, in *Œuvres complètes* (Paris, 1980).

67 Patrick Tort, *La Raison classificatoire* (Paris, 1989), p. 539.

68 Weber, *Max Weber*, p. 196.

69 Ibid., p. 235.

70 *From Max Weber: Essays in Sociology*, pp. 28ff.

71 Mitzman, *The Iron Cage*.

72 'Ce que les hommes nomment amour est bien petit, bien restreint et bien faible, comparé à cette ineffable orgie, à cette sainte prostitution de l'âme qui se donne tout entière, poésie et charité, à l'imprévu qui se montre, à l'inconnu qui passe.' Baudelaire, 'Les Foules', from 'Le Spleen de Paris', XII.

73 Max Weber, *Economy and Society*, I, p. 461.

74 'Qui ne sait pas peupler sa solitude, ne sait non plus être seul dans une foule affairée.' Baudelaire, 'Les Foules', from 'Le Spleen de Paris', XII, p. 47.

75 '. . . la possibilité de soulager et de vaincre, pendant toute votre vie, cette bizarre affection de l'Ennui, qui est la source de toutes vos maladies et de tous vos misérables progrès . . . vous régnerez sur vos vulgaires semblables; vous serez fourni de flatterieset même d'adorations; l'argent, l'or, les diamants, les palais féeriques, viendront vous chercher et vous prieront de les accepter, sans que vous ayez fait un effort pour les gagner.' Baudelaire, 'Le joueur généreux', from 'Le Spleen de Paris', XXIX, p. 110.

76 Charles Baudelaire, 'Au Lecteur', *Oeuvres complètes*, ed. Robert Laffont (Paris, 1992), p. 190.

77 Baudelaire, 'Le Spleen de Paris', *Oeuvres complètes*, p. 190.

78 Weber, *Max Weber*, p. 235.

79 Mitzman, *The Iron Cage*, pp. 144 and 249.

80 Jaspers, 'Max Weber: Politician, Scientist, Philosopher (1932)', p. 36.

81 Karl Jaspers, 'Max Weber: Concluding Characterization (1960–1961)', in Jaspers, *On Max Weber*, p. 156. The original can be found in Jaspers, *Die Grossen Philosophen Nachlass*, ed. Hans Saner (Munich, 1981), vol. 1, pp. 641–51.

82 Hannah Arendt/Karl Jaspers, *Briefwechsel, 1926–1969*, ed. Lotte Köhler and Hans Saner (Munich, 1985), pp. 671–3. Quoted in Jaspers, *On Max Weber*, pp. 186–7.

83 This question does not appear in the printed version, but was written to John Dreijmanis by Weber's nephew Eduard Baumgarten in a letter dated 1 April 1978. 'Introduction' to Jaspers, *On Max Weber*, p. xx.

84 Ibid, p. xxiv.

85 Weber, *Max Weber*, p. 330.

86 Emil Krapelin, *Manic-depressive Insanity and Paranoia* (Edinburgh, 1921), p. 75.

87 Weber, *Max Weber*, p. 54.

88 Ibid., pp. 202–6.

89 Krapelin, *Manic-depressive Insanity and Paranoia*, p. 82.

90 The first edition of the *Allgemeine Psychopathologie* is from 1913. This quotation is from the enlarged 1946 edition; see *General Psychopathology*, trans. J. Hoenig and M. W. Hamilton (Baltimore, MD, 1997), vol. II, pp. 596–7.

91 Weber, *Max Weber*, p. 690.

THREE

Benjamin and Ennui

1 'Engel (sagt man) wüssten oft nicht, ob sie unter/ Lebenden gehn oder Toten. Die ewige Strömung/ reisst durch beide Bereiche alle Alter/ immer mit sich und übertönt sie in beiden. // Schliesslich brauchen sie uns nicht mehr, die Früheentrückten,/ man entwöhnt sich des Irdischen sanft, wie man den Brüsten/

milde der Mutter entwächst. Aber wir, die so grosse/ Gehemnisse brauchen, denen aus Trauer so oft/ seliger Fortschritt entspringt –: *könnten* wir sein ohne sie?'

2 Gershom Scholem, *Walter Benjamin: The Story of a Friendship* (New York, 2003).

3 Quoted by Irving Wohlfarth, 'Resentment Begins at Home: Nietzsche, Benjamin, and the University', in *Walter Benjamin: Critical Essays and Recollections*, ed. Gary Smith (Cambridge, MA, 1988), pp. 229–30.

4 V. I. Lenin, *Materialism and Empirio-criticism*, Chapter Four, 4. Hans Cornelius was in reality a jovial bohemian, an unconventional character who painted and composed music, and as a professor defended Enlightenment and Neo-Kantian philosophy; he was very individualistic, pragmatic and passionately anti-metaphysical. See the comments on him in Susan Buck-Morss, *The Origin of Negative Dialectics: Theodor W. Adorno, Walter Benjamin, and the Frankfurt Institute* (New York, 1977).

5 Momme Brodersen, *Walter Benjamin: A Biography* (London, 1996), p. 149, *Walter Benjamin: An Intellectual Biography* (Detroit, MI, 1991), p. 86.

6 'Agesilaus Santander' (1933), reproduced in its two versions by Gershom Scholem in *Benjamin et son ange* (Paris, 1995), pp. 92–9.

7 Hannah Arendt, *Men in Dark Times* (New York, 1968). Susan Sontag, *Under the Sign of Saturn* (New York, 1980). In a biography of Benjamin published after the publication in Spanish of this book (Howard Eiland and Michael W. Jennings, *Walter Benjamin: A Critical Life*, pp. 3–4), the authors state that it is 'misleading to characterize him, as certain English-language treatments have done, as a purely saturnine and involuted figure'; they recognize that he was 'plagued by long bouts of immobilizing depression', but conclude that 'to treat Walter Benjamin as a hopeless melancholic is to caricature and reduce him.' The authors, however, continue to portray him as a philosopher lost in the mist.

8 P. S. Laplace, *Essai philosophique sur les probabilités* (Paris, 1814).

9 'Fate and Character', written in 1919 and published in 1921. *Walter Benjamin, Selected Writings* (Cambridge, MA, 2002), vol. I, pp. 201–6.

10 In the metaphor used by Edward Lorenz, it is a tornado in Texas, in his famous 1979 paper: 'Predictability: Does the Flap of a Butterfly's Wings in Brazil Set Off a Tornado in Texas?', speech at the American Association for the Advancement of Science, Washington, DC, 29 December 1979.

11 David Ruelle, *Hasard et chaos* (Paris, 1991), pp. 31–6. In reality, according to Ruelle, the mathematical proof for this situation has never been found.

12 Benjamin, 'Fate and Character', p. 202.

13 Ibid., p. 204.

14 Rainer Maria Rilke, *Duino Elegies*, trans. Stephen Cohn (Manchester, 1989), p.21.

15 Bernd Witte, *Walter Benjamin: An Intellectual Biography* (Detroit, MI, 1991), p. 51.

16 I am using the English trans. by Stanley Corngold: 'Goethe's Elective Affinities', in Walter Benjamin, *Selected Writings*, vol. I (Cambridge, MA, 1996), p. 305.

17 Ibid., p. 304.

18 The essay is dedicated to Jula Cohn, the sister of one of his childhood friends, with whom Benjamin tried to establish a relationship. For her part, Dora was in a relationship with a friend of the couple, Ernst Schoen (Brodersen, *Walter Benjamin: A Biography*, p. 127).

19 'Goethe's Elective Affinities', p. 319.

20 Ibid., p. 309.

21 Ibid., p. 332.

22 Ibid., p. 307.

23 Walter Benjamin, *The Arcades Project*, trans. Howard Eiland and Kevin McLaughlin (Cambridge, MA, 1999), D1, 3.

24 Ibid., D1, 6.

25 Giorgio de Chirico, *Memorie della mia vita* (Milan, 1962), p. 65.

26 Ibid., p. 65.

27 Benjamin, *The Arcades Project*, D8, 1.

28 There was also an English trans.: *Elective Affinities* (London, 1785). See a commentary in A. G. Steer, Jr, *Goethe's Elective Affinities: The Robe of Nessus* (Heidelberg, 1990).

29 Benjamin, 'On Language as Such and the Human Language', in *Selected Writings*, vol. I (Cambridge, MA, 1996), p. 73.

30 Benjamin, 'Central Park', in *Selected Writings*, vol. IV (Cambridge, MA, 1996), § 16. p. 170.

31 Ibid., § 17, p. 171.

32 *The Arcades Project*, M1, 6.

33 Ibid., M4a, 1. See the account of his first two experiences with the drug in 'On Hashish', trans. Howard Eiland and others, in Eiland and Michael W. Jennings, *Walter Benjamin: A Critical Life* (Cambridge, MA, 2014), p. 47 and 57.

34 Benjamin, 'Travel Souvenirs', in 'One-way Street', *Selected Writings*, vol. I (Cambridge, MA, 1996), pp. 471.

35 'Central Park', § 16.

36 Scholem, *Walter Benjamin*, p. 199.

37 Ibid., pp. 150–62.

38 Ibid., p. 162.

39 Brodersen, *Walter Benjamin*, pp. 172–6.

40 Scholem, *Walter Benjamin*, p. 198. Letter of 25 March 1929.

41 Walter Benjamin, *The Origin of German Tragic Drama*, trans. John Osborne, Introduction by George Steiner (London, 1977), p. 138.

42 Max Pensky, *Melancholy Dialectics: Walter Benjamin and the Play of Mourning* (Amherst, MA, 1993).

43 Benjamin, *The Origin of German Tragic Drama*, p. 56.

44 Ibid., pp. 138–9.

45 Ibid., p. 224.

46 Ibid., p. 139.

47 Ibid., pp. 183–4.

48 Susan Buck-Morss, *The Dialectics of Seeing: Walter Benjamin and the Arcades Project* (Cambridge, MA, 1991), pp. 175–6.

49 Pensky, *Melancholy Dialectics*, p. 138.

50 *The Origin of German Tragic Drama*, p. 149.

51 Theodor W. Adorno, 'Caracterización de Walter Benjamin' [1950], in *Sobre Walter Benjamin* (Madrid, 2001), p. 14.

52 *The Origin of German Tragic Drama*, p. 149.

53 Pensky, *Melancholy Dialectics*, p. 109.

54 Witte, *Walter Benjamin: An Intellectual Biography*, p. 83.

55 *The Origin of German Tragic Drama*, p. 235.

56 Sigmund Freud, 'Mourning and Melancholia', in *Murder, Mourning and Melancholia* (London).

57 *The Origin of German Tragic Drama*, pp. 157–8.

58 Victor Hugo, *William Shakespeare* [1864] (Paris, 1973), p. 198.

59 Freud, 'Mourning and Melancholia'.

60 Walter Benjamin, 'Left-wing Melancholy (On Erich Kästner's New Book of Poems)' [1931], trans. Ben Brewster, *Screen*, xv/2 (1974), pp. 29–31.

61 As described by Gustav Hartlaub, at the time director of the Mannheim museum. Quoted by Peter Gay in *Weimar Culture: The Outsider as Insider* (New York, 1968), p. 122.

62 Quoted in Witte, *Walter Benjamin*, p. 118.

63 'On voit un chiffonier qui vient, hochant la tête,/ Butant, et se cognant aux murs comme un poète.' Charles Baudelaire, 'Le Vin du chiffonier', from 'Les Fleurs du mal', cv, in *Œuvres complètes* (Paris, 1980).

64 Pensky, *Melancholy Dialectics*, pp. 149 and 268, n57. He also attributes the concept to a non-existent Spanish Baroque playwright. Benjamin does not mention Gracián, but takes the information from Karl Borinski, who in *Die Antike in Poetic und Kunsttheorie* (Leipzig, 1924, vol. i, p. 191) refers to the works of Baltasar Gracián published in Barcelona in 1669. Gracián also had Lorenzo as a first name, which led to Pensky's confusión when he attributes the 'mysterious contemplation' to one Lorenzo Gracian Barcellona.

65 Baltasar Gracián, 'Agudeza y arte de ingenio', in *Obras completas*, ii (Madrid, 1993). Discourses vi and xi are devoted to mysterious contemplation.

66 Ibid., p. 355, Discourse vi.

67 Ibid., pp. 356–7. Borinski refers to the cicada in the music competition.

68 Annie Cohen-Solal, *Sartre: A Life* (New York, 2005), p. 112.

69 George Howard Bauer makes a good analysis of melancholy in *La Nausée* in *Sartre and the Artist* (Chicago, il, 1969), Chapter Two.

70 Jean-Paul Sartre, 'Carnet Dupuis' [before 1935], section vi, 'De l'ennui', in *Œuvres romanesques* (Paris, 1981), p. 1684.

71 See Baudelaire, 'Les Fleurs du mal', poems lxxvi and lxxvii.

72 Walter Benjamin, 'Paris, the Capital of the Nineteenth Century', in *Selected Writings*, vol. iii (Cambridge, ma, 1996), p. 39.

73 Ibid., p. 41.
74 Letter from Adorno dated 5 June 1935. Theodor W. Adorno and Walter Benjamin, *The Complete Correspondence*, 1928–40 (Cambridge, MA, 1999), p. 93.
75 Letter from Adorno, 10 November 1938, ibid., p. 285.
76 *The Arcades Project*, J66, 1.
77 Ibid., J56a,10 and J62a, 2.
78 Ibid., J66a, 4 and 'Central Park', §4, §5.
79 Ibid., J66a,4, and 'Central Park', §4, §5. 78 G.W.F. Hegel, *The Phenomenology of Mind*, trans. J. B. Baillie (London, 1931), p. 6. Hegel explains that ennui comes from the 'shapeless repetition of one and the same idea', even if it acquires the tedious appearance of diversity. This is a monochrome and monotonous formalism that is unable to change the whole, and instead busies itself with frivolous strange and curious things that in reality reveal a naive vacuity of knowledge.
80 *The Arcades Project*, J67a, 6.
81 Ibid., J67, 2.
82 Walter Benjamin, 'On the Concept of History', thesis 1, in *Selected Writings*, vol. IV (Cambridge, MA, 1996), p. 389.
83 Rilke, *Fourth Duino Elegy*. See the comments by Kurt Wergel, 'Rilke's Fourth Duino Elegy and Kleist's Essay Über das Marionettentheater', *Modern Language Notes*, 60 (1945), pp. 73–8; Kathleen L. Komar, *Transcending Angels: Rainer Maria Rilke's Duino Elegies* (Lincoln, NE, 1987), pp. 10–37; Ursula Franklin, 'The Angel in Valéry and Rilke', *Comparative Literature*, 35 (1983), pp. 215–46.
84 Alain Montandon, 'L'Ange et l'automate chez Jean-Paul', in Henry Corbin et al., *L'Ange et l'Homme* (Paris, 1978). As a young man, Jean-Paul Richter, influenced by Leibniz, had written about some angels more immersed in the mechanicist, optimistic spirit of the Enlightenment: 'in a world where everything is linked by cause and effect, predicting the future demands nothing more than an exact knowledge of the current state of the innumerable things that play a role . . . An angel is therefore able exactly to predict events that will happen in a thousand years, since all that is needed is knowledge of the configuration of the relevant causes. If I know the cause,

I know the effect.' Quoted by Alain Montandon from the *Spiritual Exercises of Jean-Paul*, pp. 174–5.

85 Letter from Rilke to Witold Hulewicz on 13 November 1925.

86 Thesis 9 from 'Concept of History', III: quoted in Witte, *Walter Benjamin*, p. 203.

87 See especially the four final paragraphs of the stimulating and moving essay by Gershom Scholem, *Benjamin et son ange*. In it, he writes: 'l'ange de l'histoire est, au fond, une figure mélancolique' – 'the angel of history is, fundamentally, a melancholy figure'; and 'Si on peut parler d'un génie de Benjamin, il fut concentré en cet ange, et la vie de Benjamin elle-même se déroula dans la lumière saturnienne' – 'If one can speak of Benjamin's genius, it is concentrated in this angel, and Benjamin's life itself took place beneath its saturnine light' (pp. 149 and 151). In his work *Angelus Novus* (1920), Paul Klee in fact intended to represent Hitler, and what Benjamin interpreted as a heap of ruins is rather the result of the oil transfer technique the artist was beginning to adopt. See the book by Carl Djerassi, *Four Jews on Parnasus – A Conversation: Benjamin, Adorno, Scholem, Schönberg* (New York, 2008).

88 Benjamin, 'On the Concept of History', thesis 5, *Selected Writings*, p. 390.

89 See a stimulating reflection on these *vanitas* in Julián Gállego, *Visión y símbolos en la pintura española del Siglo de Oro* (Madrid, 1987), pp. 204–12.

90 'On the Concept of History', thesis 10, *Selected Writings*, p. 393.

91 Ibid., thesis 7, p. 391.

92 Ibid.

93 This is Michel Löwy's interpretation in *Walter Benjamin. Avertissement d'incendie. Une lecture des thèses 'Sur le concept d'histoire'* (Paris, 2001), p. 56.

94 *The Origin of German Tragic Drama*, p. 155.

95 See a broad explanation of this topic in my book *Melancholy and Culture: Diseases of the Soul in Golden Age Spain* (Cardiff, 2008), especially pp. 22ff and 170ff.

96 *The Origin of German Tragic Drama*, p. 157. He also observes that Abû Maˇsar believed in the 'faithfulness in love' of the saturnine character.

97 *Gesammelte Schriften* (Frankfurt, 1972), III, p. 214, quoted by Andras Sandor, 'Rilke's and Walter Benjamin's Conceptions of Rescue and Liberation', in F. Baron, E. S. Dick and W. A. Maurer, eds, *Rilke: The Alchemy of Alienation* (Lawrence, KS, 1980), p. 229.

98 Edgar Allan Poe, 'Maelzel's Chess Player', in *Essays and Reviews*, vol. XX (New York, 1984), pp. 1253–76.

99 'On the Concept of History', thesis 2, *Selected Writings*, p. 390.

100 Theodor W. Adorno, 'Introducción a los Escritos de Benjamin' [1955], in *Sobre Walter Benjamin* (Madrid, 2001), p. 37.

101 *The Origin of German Tragic Drama*, p. 166.

102 *The Arcades Project*, K1a, 8.

103 Walter Benjamin, 'Dream Kitsch', *Selected Writings*, vol. II (Cambridge, MA, 1996). See the interesting essay by Ricardo Iberlucía, *Onirokitsch: Walter Benjamin y el surrealismo* (Buenos Aires, 1998).

104 Diderot explains in this way the genius of a painter as coarse and ignorant as Carle Vanloo, whose painting *Saint Gregory Dictating His Homilies* seems to him sublime (*Salon de 1765*, ed. Else Marie Bukdahl and Annette Lorenceau, Paris, 1984, p. 47).

105 *The Arcades Project*, D1, 5; D2, 8.

106 Pierre Janet, *De l'angoisse à l'extase. Études sur les croyances et les sentiments* (Paris, 1926), vol. II, part 2, I, 2.

107 *The Arcades Project*, J69, 5.

108 'On the Concept of History', thesis 18, *Selected Writings*, p. 397.

109 Arendt, *Men in Dark Times*, p. 171.

110 Hannah Arendt says that Benjamin's death so shocked the Francoist police that they authorized his friends to continue their journey; Arendt, *Men in Dark Times* (New York, 1968).

Bibliography

Adorno, Theodor W., 'Caracterización de Walter Benjamin' [1950],
in *Sobre Walter Benjamin* (Madrid, 2001)
——, 'Introducción a los Escritos de Benjamin' [1955], in *Sobre Walter
Benjamin* (Madrid, 2001)
——, and Walter Benjamin, *The Complete Correspondence, 1928–40*
(Cambridge, MA, 1999)
Arendt, Hannah, *Men in Dark Times* (New York, 1968)
Bartra, Roger, *El Siglo de Oro de la melancolía. Textos españoles y
novohispanos sobre las enfermedades del alma* (México, 1998)
——, *Melancholy and Culture: Diseases of the Soul in Golden Age Spain*
(Cardiff, 2008)
——,*The Imaginary Networks of Political Power: A New Revised and
Expanded Edition* (Mexico, 2012)
Baudelaire, Charles, 'Les Fleurs du mal', in *Œuvres complètes* (Paris, 1980)
——, 'Le Spleen de Paris (Petits poèmes en prose)', in *Œuvres complètes*
(Paris, 1980)
Bauer, George Howard, *Sartre and the Artist* (Chicago, IL, 1969)
Baxter, Richard, *The Saints' Everlasting Rest* (New York, 1850)
Bell, Daniel, *The Cultural Contradictions of Capitalism* (New York, 1976)
Benjamin, Walter, 'Left-wing Melancholy (On Erich Kästner's New
Book of Poems)' [1931], trans. Ben Brewster, *Screen*, XV/2 (1974)
——, *The Origin of German Tragic Drama*, trans. John Osborne,
Introduction by George Steiner (London, 1977)
——, 'Central Park', in *Selected Writings*, vol. IV (Cambridge, MA, 1996)
——, 'Goethe's Elective Affinities', trans. Stanley Corngold, in *Selected
Writings*, vol. I (Cambridge, MA, 1996)
——, 'On the Concept of History', in *Selected Writings*, vol. IV
(Cambridge, MA, 1996)

——, 'On Language as Such and the Human Language', in *Selected Writings*, vol. I (Cambridge, MA, 1996)

——, 'Paris, the Capital of the Nineteenth Century', in *Selected Writings*, vol. III (Cambridge, MA, 1996)

——,'Travel Souvenirs', in *One-way Street: Selected Writings*, vol. I (Cambridge, MA, 1996)

——, *The Arcades Project*, trans. Howard Eiland and Kevin McLaughlin (Cambridge, MA, 1999)

——, 'Dream Kitsch', in *Selected Writings*, vol. II (Cambridge, MA, 2002)

——, 'Fate and Character', in *Selected Writings*, vol. I (Cambridge, MA, 2002)

Berlin, Isaiah, *The Magus of the North: J. G. Hamann and the Origins of Modern Irrationalism*, ed. Henry Hardy (London, 1993)

——, *The Roots of Romanticism* (Princeton, NJ, 1999)

Borowski, Ludwig Ernst, *Relato de la vida y el carácter de Immanuel Kant* [*Darstellung des Lebens und des Charakters Immanuel Kants*, Königsberg, 1804] (Madrid, 1993)

Brandt, Reinhardt, 'Kant en Königsberg', in *Immanuel Kant: política, derecho y antropología* (Mexico, 2001)

Brodersen, Momme, *Walter Benjamin: A Biography* (London, 1996)

Buck-Morss, Susan, *The Origin of Negative Dialectics: Theodor W. Adorno, Walter Benjamin, and the Frankfurt Institute* (New York, 1977)

——, *The Dialectics of Seeing: Walter Benjamin and the Arcades Project* (Cambridge, MA, 1991)

Burke, Edmund, *A Philosophical Enquiry into the Origin of Our Ideas of the Sublime and Beautiful*, ed. James T. Boulton (Oxford, 1987)

Cassirer, Ernst, *Language and Myth*, trans. Susanne K. Langer (New York, 1953)

——, *Kant's Life and Thought*, trans. James Haden (New Haven, CT, 1981)

Chirico, Giorgio de, *Memorie della mia vita* (Milan, 1962)

Claudel, Paul, 'Notes sur les anges' [*Présence et prophétie*], in *Œuvres complètes*, vol. XX (Paris, 1963), pp. 370–431

Cohen-Solal, Annie, *Sartre: A Life* (New York, 2005)

Creuzer, Friedrich, *Sileno, Idea y validez del simbolismo antiguo* (Barcelona, 1991)

Diderot, Denis, *Salon de 1765*, ed. Else Marie Bukdahl and Annette Lorenceau (Paris, 1984)

Diggins, John Patrick, *Max Weber: Politics and the Spirit of Tragedy* (New York, 1996)

Djerassi, Carl, *Four Jews on Parnasus – A Conversation: Benjamin, Adorno, Scholem, Schönberg* (New York, 2008)

Duque, Félix, 'Introducción' to the Spanish trans. of Friedrich Creuzer's *Sileno. Idea y validez del simbolismo antiguo* (Barcelona, 1991)

Durkeim, Émile, *Le Suicide* (Paris, 1930)

Eiland, Howard, and Michael W. Jennings, *Walter Benjamin: A Critical Life* (Cambridge, MA, 2014)

Engels, Frederick, 'Introduction to *Socialism: Utopian and Scientific*', in *Karl Marx Frederick Engels Collected Works*, vol. XXVII (New York, 1990), pp. 278–302

——, 'Ludwig Feuerbach and the End of Classical German Philosophy', in *Karl Marx Frederick Engels Collected Works*, vol. XXVI (New York, 1990), pp. 353–98

Franklin, Ursula, 'The Angel in Valéry and Rilke', *Comparative Literature*, 35 (1983), pp. 215–46

Freud, Sigmund, 'Mourning and Melancholia', in *Murder, Mourning and Melancholia* (London, 2005)

Gállego, Julián, *Visión y símbolos en la pintura española del Siglo de Oro* (Madrid, 1987)

Gay, Peter, *Weimar Culture: The Outsider as Insider* (New York, 1968)

——, *The Bourgeois Experience: Victoria to Freud* (Oxford, 1984)

Gershom, Scholem, *Walter Benjamin: The Story of a Friendship* (New York, 2003)

Godwin, Francis, *The Man in the Moone: or, a Discourse of a Voyage Thither by Domingo Gonsales, the Speedy Messenger* (London, 1638)

Goethe, Johann Wolfgang, *Elective Affinities*, trans. R. J. Hollingdale (London, 2005)

Gracián, Baltasar, 'Agudeza y arte de ingenio', in *Obras completas*, II (Madrid, 1993)

Green, Martin, *The von Richthofen Sisters: The Triumphant and the Tragic Modes of Love. Else and Frieda von Richthofen, Otto Gross, Max Weber, and D. H. Lawrence, in the Years 1870–1970* (Albuquerque, NM, 1974)

——, *Mountain of Truth: The Counterculture Begins: Ascona, 1900–1920* (Hanover, NE, 1986)

Gross, Otto, *Die cerebrale Sekundärfunction* (Leipzig, 1902)

Gulyga, Arsenij, *Immanuel Kant: His Life and Thought* (Boston, MA, 1987)

Gumbrecht, H. U., *Production of Presence* (Stanford, CA, 2004)

——, *Our Broad Present: Time and Contemporary Culture* (New York, 2014)

Haverkamp, Anselm, *Leaves of Mourning: Hölderlin's Late Work* (Albany, NY, 1995)

Hegel, G.W.F., *The Phenomenology of Mind*, trans. J. B. Baillie (London, 1931)

Hugo, Victor, *William Shakespeare* [1864] (Paris, 1973)

Iberlucía, Ricardo, *Onirokitsch: Walter Benjamin y el surrealismo* (Buenos Aires, 1998)

Jachmann, Reinhold Bernhard, *Emmanuel Kant raconté dans des lettres à un ami*, trans. Jean Mostler, in *Kant intime* (Paris, 1985)

James, William, *The Letters of William James* (Boston, MA, 1920)

Janet, Pierre, *De l'angoisse à l'extase. Études sur les croyances et les sentiments* (Paris, 1926)

Jaspers, Karl, 'Max Weber: Politician, Scientist, Philosopher (1932)', in Karl Jaspers, *On Max Weber* (New York, 1989)

——, *General Psychopathology*, trans. J. Hoenig and M. W. Hamilton (Baltimore, MD, 1997)

Kant, Immanuel, *Crítica del juicio*, trans. Alejo García Moreno and Juan Rovira (Madrid, 1876)

——, *Antropología práctica (según el manuscrito inédito de C. C. Mrongovius, 1785)*, trans. Roberto Rodríguez Aramayo (Madrid, 1990)

——, *Dreams of a Spirit-seer Elucidated by Dreams of Metaphysics: Cambridge Edition of the Works of Immanuel Kant, Theoretical Philosophy, 1755–1770*, trans. and ed. David Walford (Cambridge, 1992)

——, *Critique of the Power of Judgment*, trans. Paul Guyer and Eric Matthews (Cambridge, 2000)

——, 'Anthropology from a Practical Point of View', in *The Cambridge Edition of the Works of Immanuel Kant: Anthropology, History and Education*, ed. Günter Zöller and Robert B. Louden (Cambridge, 2007)

——, 'Essay on the Maladies of the Head', in *The Cambridge Edition of the Works of Immanuel Kant: Anthropology, History and Education* (Cambridge, 2011)

——, *Observations on the Feeling of the Beautiful and Sublime and Other Writings*, ed. Patrick Frierson and Paul Guyer (Cambridge, 2011)

King III, John Owen, *The Iron of Melancholy: Structures of Political Conversion in America from the Puritan Conscience to Victorian Neurosis* (Middletown, CT, 1983)

Komar, Kathleen L., *Transcending Angels: Rainer Maria Rilke's Duino Elegies* (Lincoln, NE, 1987)

Kraepelin, Emil, *Manic-depressive Insanity and Paranoia* (Edinburgh, 1921)

Kuehn, Manfred, *Kant: A Biography* (Cambridge, 2001)

Laplace, P. S., *Essai philosophique sur les probabilités* (Paris, 1814)

Lenin, V. I., *Materialism and Empirio-criticism* (Moscow, 1970)

Lepenies, Wolf, *Melancholy and Society*, trans. J. Gaines and D. Jones (Cambridge, MA, 1992)

Lévi-Strauss, Claude, *Tristes Tropiques* (Paris, 1955)

Lichtblau, Klaus, 'The Protestant Ethic versus the "New Ethic"', in *Weber's Protestant Ethic: Origins, Evidence, Contexts*, ed. Hartmut Lehmann and Guenther Roth (Cambridge, 1993)

Lieburg, M. J. van, *The Disease of the Learned: A Chapter from the History of Melancholy and Hypochondria* (Oss, Netherlands, 1990)

Lorenz, Edward, 'Predictability: Does the Flap of a Butterfly's Wings in Brazil Set Off a Tornado in Texas?', speech at the American Association for the Advancement of Science, Washington, DC, 29 December 1979

Löwy, Michel, *Walter Benjamin. Avertissement d'incendie. Une lecture des thèses 'Sur le concept d'histoire'* (Paris, 2001)

Lyotard, Jean-François, *La Condition postmoderne. Rapport sur le savoir* (Paris, 1979)

——, *Leçons sur l'analytique du sublime* (Paris, 1991)

MacKinnon, Malcolm H., 'Part I: Calvinism and the Infallible Assurance of Grace' and 'Part II: Weber's Exploration of Calvinism', *British Journal of Sociology*, 39 (1988), pp. 143–77 and 178–210

——, 'The Longevity of the Thesis: A Critique of the Critics', in *Weber's Protestant Ethic: Origins, Evidence, Contexts*, ed. Hartmut Lehmann and Guenther Roth (Cambridge, 1993)

Milton, John, *Il Penseroso and The Allegro* (with paintings by William Blake) (New York, 1954)

Mitzman, Arthur, *The Iron Cage: An Historical Interpretation of Max Weber* (New York, 1970)

Montandon, Alain, 'L'Ange et l'automate chez Jean-Paul', in Henry
  Corbin et al., *L'Ange et l'Homme* (Paris, 1978)

More, Henry, *Enthusiasmus Triumphatus, or, A Discourse of the Nature,
  Causes, Kinds, and Cure of Enthusiasme* (London, 1662)

Otto, Rudolf, *Le Sacré*, trans. André Jundt (Paris, 1995)

Pensky, Max, *Melancholy Dialectics: Walter Benjamin and the Play
  of Mourning* (Amherst, MA, 1993)

Poe, Edgar Allan, 'Maelzel's Chess Player', in *Essays and Reviews*,
  vol. XX (New York, 1984), pp. 1253–76

Printz, Othon, *Mélancolie et confession religieuse. Étude
  statistique, clinique et psychopathologique*, thesis no. 85
  (Strasbourg, 1966)

Quincey, Thomas de, *The Last Days of Kant* [1827] (Edinburgh, 1863)

Radden, Jennifer, *The Nature of Melancholy* (Oxford, 2000)

Rilke, Rainer Maria, 'Letter to Witold Hulewicz, November 13, 1925',
  quoted in Rilke's *Obras*, bilingual edn, trans. José María Valverde
  (Barcelona, 1967), p. 264

Rubin, Julius H., *Religious Melancholy and Protestant Experience
  in America* (Oxford, 1994)

Ruelle, David, *Hasard et chaos* (Paris, 1991)

Sandor, Andras, 'Rilke's and Walter Benjamin's Conceptions
  of Rescue and Liberation', in *Rilke: The Alchemy of Alienation*
  F. Baron, E. S. Dick and W. A. Maurer (Lawrence, KS, 1980)

Sartre, Jean-Paul, 'Carnet Dupuis' [before 1935], section VI, 'De l'ennui',
  in *Œuvres romanesques* (Paris, 1981)

Scarborough, Milton, *Myth and Modernity: Postcritical Reflections*
  (Albany, NY, 1994)

Schiller, Friedrich von, 'On the Sublime', in *Two Essays*, trans. Julius
  A. Elias (New York, 1966)

Scholem, Gershom, *Benjamin et son ange* (Paris, 1995)

——, *Walter Benjamin: The Story of a Friendship* (New York, 2003)

Schwentker, Wolfgang, 'Passion as a Mode of Life: Max Weber,
  the Otto Gross Circle and Eroticism', in *Max Weber and
  His Contemporaries*, ed. Wolfgang J. Mommsen and Jürgen
  Osterhammel (London, 1987)

Scriblerus, Martinus, *Peri Bathos: Of the Art of Sinking in Poetry,
  Written in the Year MDCCXXVII*, in *The Works of Alexander Pope*,
  ed. Joseph Warton, vol. VI (London, 1803)

Sena, John F., 'Melancholic Madness and the Puritans', *Harvard Theological Review*, LXVI/3 (1973), pp. 293–309

Shell, Susan Meld, *The Embodiment of Reason: Kant on Spirit, Generation, and Community* (Chicago, IL, 1996)

Shenk, Joshua Wolf, *Lincoln's Melancholy: How Depression Challenged a President and Fueled his Greatness* (Boston, MA, 2006)

Sontag, Susan, *Under the Sign of Saturn* (New York, 1980)

Steer, Jr, A. G. *Goethe's Elective Affinities: The Robe of Nessus* (Heidelberg, 1990)

Tort, Patrick, *La Raison classificatoire* (Paris, 1989)

Wasianski, Ehrgott André Ch., *Emmanuel Kant dans les Dernières Années*, trans. Jean Mostler, in *Kant intime* (Paris, 1985)

Weber, Marianne, *Max Weber: A Biography*, trans. and ed. Harry Zohn (New York, 1975)

Weber, Max, 'Science as a Vocation', in *From Max Weber: Essays in Sociology*, ed. and trans. H. H. Gerth and C. Wright Mills (New York, 1958)

——, *Economy and Society: An Outline of Interpretive Sociology* (Berkeley, CA, 1978)

——, 'Prospects of Democracy in Tsarist Russia', in *Selections in Translation*, ed. W. G. Runciman (Cambridge, 1978)

——, *The Protestant Ethic and the Spirit of Capitalism*, trans. Talcott Parsons (Los Angeles, CA, 1998)

Wergel, Kurt, 'Rilke's Fourth Duino Elegy and Kleist's Essay Über das Marionettentheater', *Modern Language Notes*, 60 (1945), pp. 73–8

Witte, Bernd, *Walter Benjamin: An Intellectual Biography* (Detroit, MI, 1991)

Wohlfarth, Irving, 'Resentment Begins at Home: Nietzsche, Benjamin, and the University', in *Walter Benjamin: Critical Essays and Recollections*, ed. Gary Smith (Cambridge, MA, 1988)

——, *Hombres del extranjero: Walter Benjamin y el Parnaso judeoalemán* (Mexico, 1999)